JOB EVALUATION
═══ AND ═══
REMUNERATION
S T R A T E G I E S

FRANS POELS

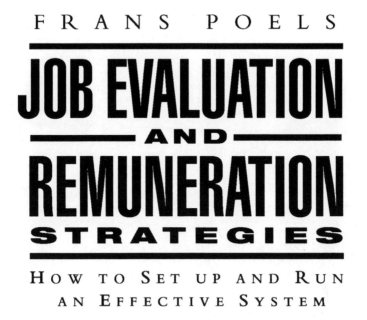

JOB EVALUATION
AND
REMUNERATION
STRATEGIES

HOW TO SET UP AND RUN
AN EFFECTIVE SYSTEM

KOGAN
PAGE

YOURS TO HAVE AND TO HOLD
BUT NOT TO COPY

First published in 1997

Kogan Page Limited
120 Pentonville Road
London N1 9JN

© Frans Poels, 1997

British Library Cataloguing in Publication Data

A CIP record for this book is available from the British Library.

ISBN 0 7494 2280 7

The masculine pronoun has been used throughout this book. This stems from a desire to avoid ugly and cumbersome language, and no discrimination, prejudice or bias is intended.

Typeset by Saxon Graphics Ltd, Derby
Printed and bound in Great Britain by Biddles Ltd, Guildford and King's Lynn

Contents

List of figures

List of tables

1

Preface

1.1 INTRODUCTION

Job evaluation and remuneration are two core aspects of the vast area of personnel management. Job evaluation is defined here as the process of examining, describing and evaluating the content of the function and ranking of related functions. Remuneration is the process which takes place after functions have been ranked and through which a salary structure will be established.

The final word on remuneration and pay is definitely not yet written or spoken. We all nurture our own beliefs and opinions, because the subject has direct personal consequences for each of us. Remuneration is an important basic ingredient of our existence as it is an essential element of our working life and governs the very existence of our organisations.

By far the greatest part of the remuneration people receive is based on job-specific pay with the weight of the job as one of the deciding factors. A systematic framework is required to manage differences in pay in such a way that they support the objectives of the organisations and result in a fair remuneration for the individuals. A host of such systems is currently available, but their workings, possibilities and limitations are unclear to many. An interesting trend is that 'employability', 'potential' and 'competencies' play an increasingly important role as a basis for remuneration. The value of the job attached to it on the basis of its weight is increased by a reward for the broader employability of the employee in multiple jobs. Also the competencies an employee demonstrates and the potential he possesses become more and more important and consequently deserve higher rewards. A major challenge is how the level of these rewards should be established.

To match the remuneration policy to the culture of the organisation and the developments in the labour market, regular comparisons must be made and the level and structure of pay must be modified where needed. The question is, how these comparisons can or should be made?

This book does not provide ready-made answers to these questions. That is neither its purpose, nor would it be possible. In order to arrive ultimately at some solutions we first of all have to master the basic techniques of job evaluation and remuneration. This book therefore presents these techniques systematically and discusses the tools for evaluating jobs, constructing a salary structure and comparing salaries.

All over the world a substantial number of methods for evaluating jobs is in use. Most of these are marketed by commercially operating organisations, but some large companies have developed their own method. Some big corporations have generated an internal system in co-operation with an external consultancy firm. Other organisations have developed an entirely separate methodology, because externally acquired methods did not match sufficiently specific views held within the organisation.

A separate approach, which in Great Britain has been adopted by Thomas Cook, is gradually to substitute 'role evaluation' for 'job evaluation'. This approach based on competence seeks to align the skills, know-how and training necessary to perform a specific function within an organisation. By determining the content of this 'role' and comparing it with the profile of the employee, it can be established to what extent he meets the requirements. Remuneration can also be tackled differently from what is customary. Instead of basing the pay on the weight of the major responsibilities and tasks of the job, an analysis is made of the required skills. Examples are:

- professional qualifications;
- attitudes;
- the ability to work in a team;
- leadership;
- communication skills.

Whatever method is used, most organisations hire job evaluation specialists. The human resource professionals generally do not perform job evaluations themselves because traditional education in the field of personnel and personnel management at college or university level unfortunately does not cover the subject of job evaluation sufficiently.

A substantial number of pay systems is based upon the weight of the job and the number of years in that job. The weight of the job is determined by means of the job evaluation system, whereas the number of years is translated in a salary band on which the basic pay is situated. This weight is calculated mainly through mathematical techniques that take into account the broader context. In contrast to other aspects of personnel management this dealing with numbers and relationships between numbers has no foundation in behavioural sciences. The purpose of these operations is to provide a quantitative basis on which policy decisions can be based. In practice these calculations and techniques remain the province of specialists.

⊙   A similar situation occurs in developing salary structures. Here, too, external firms have gained substantial expertise which may be made available to organisations. Implementing a (new) method of job evaluation or designing a salary structure is not a routine task of the personnel professional.

A salary structure is a ranked series of salary amounts distributed over a number of columns which are based on certain mathematical relationships. Without such relationships a salary structure is not able to cope with salary measures which have been agreed within the context of a policy for levelling off or rather increasing income differences. Other measures such as extending or shortening salary scales may (unintentionally) cause considerable distortions within a salary structure. A current issue, which may also create problems, is the way in which an amount below the level of the lowest salary group should be established.

Greater flexibility is called for with regard to both job evaluation and remuneration. Is it still necessary to make a formal description of each job? In the literature the concept of the 'jobless organisation' has been introduced. Is it necessary that every salary amount of each employee can be derived from the salary scale that is in use? These are recurring questions in the professional literature – also major developments are taking place in this respect. Automation is spreading and management allocation methods are being introduced. These developments too will be discussed.

Before job evaluation methods can be adopted, information on the commercially available systems needs to be collected. What are the differences between these systems? What is being measured? Broadly speaking, job evaluation methods can be divided into two main types according to the means of comparison used:

- *Non-analytical* methods in which the whole jobs are examined and compared, without being analysed into their constituent parts or elements;

- Analytical methods in which jobs are analysed by reference to one or more criteria, factors or aspects.

By far, analytical methods are the most used systems. A well-known method is the so-called *point factor method* in which the relative weight of the job is represented by a number. Comparing a function on the basis of a description of a standard job or level – so-called reasoned comparisons – has also become a common method. To help make your choice, this book compares a number of methods which are being extensively applied. This comparison will also facilitate an evaluation of the usefulness to an organisation of methods which will not be discussed in this book.

Similarly, quite a few aspects and issues concerning comparing salaries need clarification. If a pay policy needs to be developed or modified, it is important to know how competitive this policy will be in the labour market. In qualitative terms a comparative analysis of salaries – so-called salary survey – should be directed at both the pay practice and the salary policy, two items which are frequently confused. Of the two, comparing pay practices is the one used most often. The ways in which consultancy firms try to clarify and explain this analysis (usually through mathematics) may differ substantially. As a consequence the results are certainly not always comparable and need to be interpreted carefully. In addition, the quality of analyses currently available in the market needs to be improved. We therefore describe the parameters and constraints to determine the requirements of organisations and jobs to be included in these analyses as well as the requirements to be met by the firm that performs the analysis. This book aims to provide insight into the techniques on which job evaluation (Part I) and remuneration (Part II) are based and which result in a flexible pay system. To that end, first the traditional form of both elements will be discussed and then their more flexible varieties. Each part will conclude with a comparison of the major job evaluation methods and comparative analysis of salaries (salary surveys). Both comparisons provide basic information on systems that are currently available on the market.

1.2 FOR WHOM IS THIS BOOK INTENDED?

Time and again it appears that many line managers and professionals, and personnel professionals in particular, need a more broad and profound insight into the complex area of remuneration. Carefully designed training programmes on the application of job evaluation, whether or not in conjunction with the owners of systems, generally achieve only marginal results. To a large extent this is due to a too narrow perspective on job evaluation. In other cases the participants have insufficient access to relevant literature. In general, job evaluation is solely treated with the technical aspects of remuneration in mind. As a result the richness and feasibility of the issue do not become evident.

An additional problem is that the technical aspects of personnel management (which includes job evaluation, designing and developing a salary structure and comparing the pay policy of the firm with the external labour market) does not receive sufficient attention in higher education. The book is therefore intended in particular for the personnel practitioner who wants to extend his knowledge and skills of the technique of job evaluation and remuneration. The interested line manager, however, who seeks to broaden his knowledge, may find it a source of useful information,

1.3 THE FUNCTION OF JOB EVALUATION AND REMUNERATION IN PERSONNEL MANAGEMENT

Major elements of the conditions for the existence of an organisation are:

- *The rationale behind its existence.* Important questions are: Why does an organisation exist? How can an organisation survive?
- *The design.* The question to answer here is: How may the work within the organisation be divided and co-ordinated?
- *The quality of working life.* The essential question on the quality of working life is: Through which organisational measures can the organisation be made attractive to the stakeholders, and in particular to the employees, to such an extent that they want to commit themselves permanently to the organisation?

Figure 1.1 shows the role of the personnel function within the interaction of these conditions for its meaningful existence. The main reason for referring to this vision on organisations is to stress the fact that these three elements constitute the background against which the design, development and evaluation of functions and jobs and their position within the organisation must be viewed.

The relationship between design and rationale of the organisation determines the content of the job. The relationship between rationale

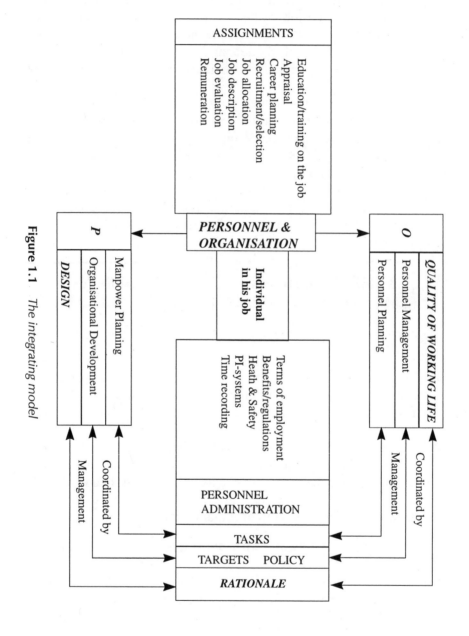

Figure 1.1 *The integrating model*

and quality of working life constitutes the basis for the pay policy. In Figure 1.1 the total scope of the personnel function is divided into two main blocks: assignments – the main tasks of the personnel function – and personnel administration – the administrative task in support of the function as such. It will be clear that both job description and job evaluation constitute different assignments. The job description needs to be separated because it is a basic function that serves other assignments and may not simply be seen as part of evaluating jobs.

On the basis of the 'integrative model' in Figure 1.1 the three elements of the existence of an organisation can be more precisely defined:

Rationale

The compilation of objectives and the strategies derived from these objectives which constitute the foundation for the design and quality of working life of the organisation.

Design

Objectives are translated into job requirements on the basis of which jobs can be constructed. The design in turn can be used for measuring the quality of working life within the organisation.

Quality of working life

Optimising the co-ordination between job, organisation and holder of the job in order to achieve the objectives of the organisation.

Figure 1.2 illustrates which aspects will be discussed. It demonstrates that the technical aspects of the human resource function are to a large extent dependent upon the opinions held in the environment of the organisation.

Thus it is important to have a proper picture of what views are held on general concepts as well as on specific subjects, in particular by consultancy firms. Ample attention will therefore be paid to the definitions of various concepts.

Numerous books and articles already exist on developing remuneration strategies, therefore the book is not intended to assist in formulating a pay policy. Its purpose is to help to translate an integrative strategy for the various functional areas into clear descriptions of jobs and departmental tasks, as well as of the characteristics of the organisation. It also provides insight into the role of job evaluation within personnel management.

The book will support the reader in making job descriptions as a starting point for analysing and evaluating jobs. To this end two different jobs – head of the personnel department and a secretary – are

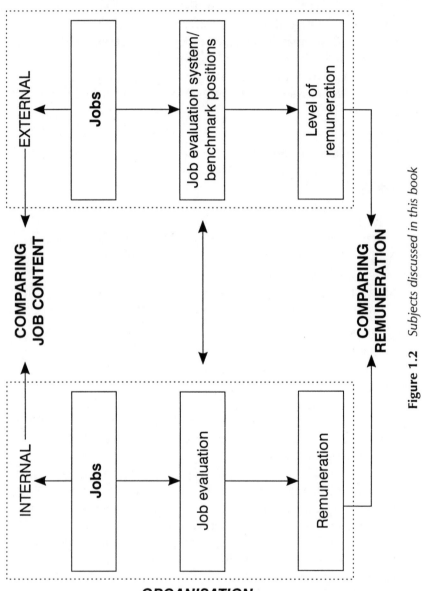

Figure 1.2 *Subjects discussed in this book*

presented; the former as an example of a supporting (policy-making) function, the latter an operational job. Both descriptions are based upon the requirements of the Hay Guide Chart and Profile Method. Next, assessment is made of the way in which methods analyse and evaluate jobs. After this practical exercise a number of job evaluation methods are discussed in more detail. With this insight the personnel officer should be able to enter a meaningful discussion on the subject with an external consultant.

Chapter 2 – Job evaluation – treats such subjects as: objectives of the study of job evaluation, procedures and education. The demand for more flexible applications of job evaluation is growing steadily. The reason is that management wants to perform job evaluation itself with only a little support from the personnel department. Job families and the job level matrix are also presented in this chapter.

The chapter on 'Remuneration' discusses the technique of building a salary scale. Central questions are: Which parameters and constraints determine the relationships within a salary scale? How can the results of a job evaluation exercise be translated into a pay policy and a salary structure?

One of the aspects which deserves close attention in formulating the pay policy is comparing this policy with the salary level in the external labour market. To illustrate this, some external salary surveys will be analysed and contrasted. What do the results of such studies tell us? Do we now know what salaries are being paid in the market?

1.3.1 General principles of a pay policy

The quality of (working) life within an organisation depends not only on having constructed jobs with, for example, some freedom for taking decisions ('empowerment'), but also on acceptable relationships between salaries. In practice the pay structure appears often to be merely decorative, like the stars and stripes on a uniform. The scale is equivalent to a 'rank' and expresses recognition and appreciation.

If employees are assigned to a lower scale as a consequence of new results from a job evaluation, for example after a major restructuring, it is not always sufficient if the pill is sweetened by maintaining the former salary (acquired rights). Frustration arises because a stripe is removed from the arm. The employee perceives that he has been demoted to a lower rank.

It can be said that generally accepted relationships in pay prevail over the absolute level of the remuneration. To the outside world the amount of the salary is usually the most important basis for comparisons of status and achievement.

In order to obtain a proper view into all aspects that influence the development of a remuneration policy, we start with a discussion of the general conditions of such a policy. In this way we avoid the situation where, in a final stage, it becomes evident that certain (obvious) issues and aspects have been omitted. In addition the connection with external studies and salary surveys will thus not been hampered, because elements which determine the level or status of the remuneration, have not been properly dealt with.

1.3.2 Conditions of a pay policy

Though the book includes a checklist for both job evaluation and remuneration it seems useful to state here some general conditions for the entire pay policy. As these conditions determine the total area of job evaluation and remuneration, they provide the background for the discussions throughout the book.

- The methodology must be logically sound and fit closely to other types of rules within the organisation.
- The internal relationships of the organisation must be reflected in the relative differences in pay which result from the established pay policy.
- The pay policy must be in accordance with what the employees perceive as fair.
- The methodology that is being constructed must comply with legal requirements and obligations, such as the conditions of the collective labour agreements, social security laws, etc.
- The pay policy must contribute to the rationale of the organisation and must be in accordance with the design and the quality of working life of the organisation. In addition it must be kept in mind that the personnel costs must never exceed what the organisation can bear.

The conditions will serve as a guideline for the discussions throughout the book.

2

Evaluating jobs

2.1 INTRODUCTION

After the Second World War job evaluation underwent profound developments. As experience in this area grew, criticism of the methods used increased as well. A scientific basis still does not exist and the whole field is under attack from academics and in particular from psychologists. Job evaluation methods, however, have evolved in practice and the embedded values and standards have been developed by trial and error. As a consequence the discipline of job evaluation is self-affirmative; it feeds on itself. Organisations are flexible and change with some regularity, which makes it difficult for job evaluation systems to remain up to date and not to inhibit further developments. The latter, though, is actually seldom the case. If we take job evaluation in a narrow sense as a form of so-called 'ascertaining job analysis', much time is wasted with repeatedly describing and evaluating jobs. However, job analysis can also be a useful tool during the starting stages of reorganisation processes if a structuring approach of job analysis is applied. The purpose of the job analysis is in this case not to record a factual situation (afterwards), but to make models and to help in shaping the desired outcome in advance; not to provide an exhaustive stock-taking of a job including as much detail as possible, but short, output-oriented job descriptions.

In tracing the development of job evaluation methods, it is interesting to note that:

- In general methods have been simplified continuously so that they are more easily understood by individual employees;
- Increasingly, system owners adapt their methods to the demands and culture of the organisations for which job analyses are carried out (customisation);
- Differences in views are clarified and are better understood;

■ Methods have been tested for their gender bias and modified accordingly;

■ The personal computer is increasingly being used to support the job evaluation process;

■ Employees increasingly demand a say in what is going on within the organisation and therefore also in the evaluation of jobs. More and more attention is being paid to the process of job evaluation and the way in which this is communicated to employees.

■ The way in which individual capabilities of employees can or should be evaluated as an element in determining pay levels is under critical scrutiny.

Though the latter issue is, in fact, separate from the evaluation of a position independent of the person, it will become a major pay factor in a growing number of organisations. The same consultancy firms that introduce job evaluation methods on the market will increasingly address the issue of how competence should be rewarded.

As a consequence of changing views on the place of human resource management within the overall strategy of the organisation, there is a trend in which line management perceives job evaluation as its 'property' and not the domain of a specialist department. However, it does not in general take the customary approach and apply expert systems by itself, but uses adapted versions of job evaluation methods. As such Job Family Systems are coming into use, but computer supported versions of job evaluation methods also assist in simplifying the practice of job evaluation. We will discuss this at a later stage. Whether these views and approaches will be generally accepted and adopted, will depend to a large extent upon the culture and the management style of organisations.

In the vast majority of organisations job evaluation will be carried out in the traditional way for a long time to come.

Job evaluation methods can roughly be divided into two large groups:

■ Methods that have been developed and introduced commercially by external firms;

■ Home-grown methods (Michael Armstrong, *Job evaluation – doing it yourself*; issue nos. 62 and 63 in Croner's Pay & Benefit Briefing, September 1994).

The advantage of external methods is that they are being applied in a large number of organisations and that they have to be flexible so that they can be adapted to the differences in organisation structure, culture, type of jobs, business processes, etc. Home-grown methods are attuned to the specific features of the individual organisation and in general do not allow for external comparisons. The advantage of internally developed methods though, is that they are more familiar to the employees and thus will be more readily accepted. As the methods of consultancy firms are being applied in different organisations, these firms can take into account developments in society and fine-tune and/or adjust their methods or improve the process of job evaluation accordingly. However, it is quite possible for home-grown methods to acquire flexibility as well. Trade unions are not particularly fond of internally developed methods, firstly because they are not always up to date and secondly because it is obviously difficult to test their suitability for the context within which they will be applied. Adequate testing criteria have not yet become available.

Job evaluation consists of the following elements:

- A clearly defined method which includes precise definitions of characteristics and entries to tables;
- Benchmark jobs that have been defined and evaluated according to the requirements of the method;
- Procedures, which clearly prescribe the course of the whole process. Careful attention needs to be paid to the appeal procedure;
- Plain, easy-to-understand communications on the method. Restraint on methods, procedures and such may cause more harm than benefit. Knowledge and insight increase the confidence of the employees.

Job evaluation is the process through which jobs are described, analysed and ultimately weighted or evaluated by means of a job evaluation method. The outcome, a total score in points, expresses the weight of a particular job in relation to other jobs. In that way a job can be ranked.

It should be noted that this outcome is only an approximation, though it is the result of a systematic procedure. Job evaluation is in fact a procedure for making a subjective (estimating) process objective. It is not a science, but an instrument that has proved its practical usefulness.

Job evaluation is thus a process which consists of several steps (see Figure 2.1). In order to duly carry out this process, these steps need to be carefully executed. Jobs are not isolated, but every job can ultimately be traced back to the objectives of the corporation.

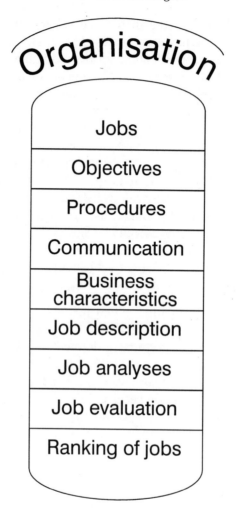

Figure 2.1   *The process of job evaluation – consecutive steps in the job evaluation process*

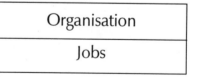

Because *jobs* or functions are part of an *organisation,* job evaluation must take all elements of the organisation into consideration; what belongs to the responsibility and authority of one department/job must not be attributed to another as well. The coherence and interrelationships should therefore be clearly established. Only then is it possible to compare and weigh functions.

Objectives

Before any investigation is started, the *objectives* of that investigation must have been unambiguously formulated. Organisations often neglect this requirement and thus have to conclude later on that the sole results of their efforts is that only the existing relationships between salaries have been established. A tedious side effect of this narrow approach is that the interest of the employees for job evaluation suffers. The embedding of the methods in personnel management as a whole, which is required for developing and maintaining such interest, is lacking. Section 2.2 discusses some applications of job evaluation that have to be considered in formulating the objectives of the process.

Procedures

The success of job evaluation depends to a large extent upon the availability of clear *procedures* (see section 2.3), as these procedures allow the employee or the union representative to know the process and to check its progress. The procedures make clear what is expected from all parties.

Procedures not only describe the course of the process, but provide information on the content of job evaluation, its methods and practices. This information is very important for the acceptance of the (results of) job evaluation.

Communication

This is why *communication* is such an essential element (see section 2.4).

The next step is obtaining information on the organisation. From the start of the investigation, the interrelationships between departments and functions within departments need to be clearly established. This avoids repeated discussions on basic responsibilities, the allocation of tasks, etc beyond the jobs and job-holders under consideration. If these issues have not been made clear on department level, how would that be possible on the level of individual jobs?

Business characteristic

The *business characteristic* is an excellent instrument for bringing clarity on the interrelationships between departments and their functions (see section 2.5).

Job description

When the interrelationships within the organisation have been identified, individual *job descriptions* can be made (see section 2.6). The procedure indicated above applies mainly to producing job descriptions.

Job analyses

A next logical step is making a job analysis based on the criteria of the method used (see section 2.7). The job analyst must be able to establish if, and to what extent, the job reflects the various criteria. The resulting document is the link between the job description and the job evaluation.

Job evaluation

With the results of the job analysis, and referring to the benchmark jobs and evaluations (as reflected in the tables and definitions of the job evaluation method), the *job evaluation*, in a more strict sense is made (see section 2.8). This evaluation determines finally the relative weight of the job.

Ranking of jobs

When all jobs have been evaluated, they can be ranked according to their weight. This *ranking* concludes the process of job evaluation (see section 2.9). Next, the final result can be used as a basis for designing a salary structure.

2.2 OBJECTIVES

In many organisations job descriptions are used exclusively to evaluate jobs (see Figure 2.2). The reason is probably that the organisation is not aware of alternative uses. Usually the purpose of the job evaluation exercise is limited to creating a basis for a pay policy. Also the assignment of an external consultancy often does not include addi-

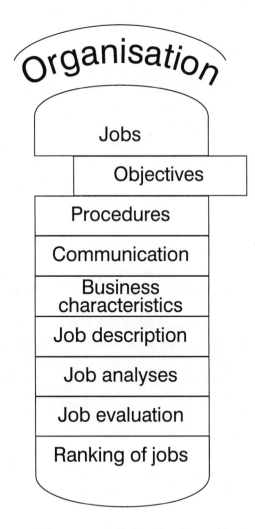

Figure 2.2 *The process of job evaluation – objectives*

tional considerations or applications. If, at a later stage, the organisation still wants to use the job description for other purposes, it is often hardly suitable or its set-up has to be modified. The latter, though, is not as difficult as it would seem. If the design of the job description is properly thought out, the description itself can be adjusted to the new demands.

The possibilities of job evaluation can only be fully exploited if the results of the weighing process are available for comparisons.

In this context it is necessary to point to the differences between a job description and a task description. First we give a definition of the job concept and of the concept task.

A *job* is a collection of tasks in conjunction with certain responsibilities and competence

---

A *task* is a collection of similar activities

The job description is therefore first of all aimed at recording the responsibilities and competence that the job contains. Information on details and task are only included as a clarification.

If we concentrate on the objectives of a job description project, we may choose from the following possibilities:

Remuneration

Remuneration is the most common purpose for which job descriptions are made. This process provides the basic information for developing a pay policy. Most remuneration systems are based on differences in the weight of jobs. Job evaluations express these relative weights in a specific ranking of the relevant jobs.

If the jobs and job levels are clustered in a well-thought-out way, we obtain job families which can be linked to salary groups (See Chapter 7 – 'Definitions').

Recruitment and selection

Recruitment and selection benefit if a proper overview of job requirements can be used. If detailed information from job evaluation has also been made available, these requirements can be substantiated to a further extent as personnel officials have insight into the level of required knowledge, social skills, etc.

Training and development

The results of the personnel evaluation can be compared with the job demands that have been established in the job descriptions. This provides insight into the gaps that have to be bridged through targeted training and development.

Personnel assessment

Job evaluation can be used for quantitative personnel review and more specifically for performance appraisals, though not for qualitative reviews. The job description records the 'contract' between the boss and the employee: what is expected of the performance of the employee in his job. It is an excellent starting point for a discussion on the shortcomings/gaps in the performance, conspicuous qualities of the employee, etc.

Career counselling and personnel planning

If employees show interest in different aspects of a similar job at a higher level, a job description is again an excellent and objective tool for examining opportunities for training and development. In this way it constitutes a sound basis for career counselling and personnel planning.

Organisational analyses

Many agree that making job descriptions is an excellent tool for becoming thoroughly familiar with an organisation. But that type of knowledge mainly concerns details. When participating in the evaluation process, insight is needed into the interrelationships between functions, or the lack of these. In this way it can be established whether a certain responsibility or competence does indeed belong only to one job and is evaluated within the context of that job. Following this line of thought, job descriptions may be used as a starting point for analysing an organisation.

A general knowledge of job evaluation and insight into the evaluation methods being used are essential for a broader approach. It makes a substantial difference whether supporting jobs or operational jobs are being evaluated. Sometimes, therefore, different methods of job evaluation are being used for different types of jobs, eg one method for higher level jobs and another for jobs at lower levels. Then, however, these different methods are not only used for remuneration issues, but for other purposes as well.

In this section job evaluation has been reviewed in a much broader context than in the following chapters. The emphasis of the book is on the technique of job evaluation and remuneration and does not intend to elaborate on other applications. Job evaluation will be discussed insofar as it is useful for designing and developing a salary structure.

Having made this choice we can proceed to the next step: the procedures required for a proper execution of the entire process of job evaluation. Procedures are important issues in the early phases of the process, as they inform the employees of what they may expect. In addition, these procedures are an important subject for discussions with (formal) representatives of the employees.

2.3 PROCEDURES

Procedures for job evaluation concern primarily two issues (see Figure 2.3):

- the implementation of the job evaluation system, and
- appealing against the outcome of job evaluation.

Like good education thorough procedures are very important to the organisation. They provide certainty to the employees with regard to their fixed salary position. In addition, they are a measure for the care and meticulousness with which the examination will be carried out. The appeal procedure is of particular importance. In most cases employees do not say what they think during the job analysis. It is only after they have been informed of the results that they give their reactions. However meticulously the analysis has been carried out, at that moment the individual employee has to know what stage he has reached and how he can appeal against the outcome of the analysis.

Depending upon the type and size of the organisation, procedures may be simple or elaborate and comprehensive. The procedure for the implementation of job evaluation should comprise some carefully defined elements.

Procedures for carrying out examinations for evaluating jobs may differ with respect to the amount of participation from both the employee concerned and his boss. The basic procedure generally boils down to the following steps:

Completing a questionnaire

Each employee whose job will be examined will be asked to complete a questionnaire. The information in this document gives

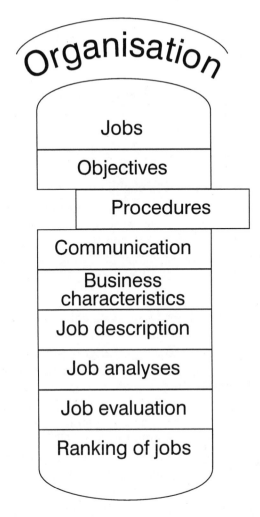

Figure 2.3 *The process of job evaluation – procedures*

some idea as to content of the job. It is also a good preparation for the subsequent interview with the job analyst. When the job description is made by the employee himself, the questionnaire is an excellent instrument to obtain the necessary information in a systematic way.

Interview with the job-holder

Next the interview is held with the holder of the job or with a representative from the holders if the same job is performed by several employees. The purpose of this interview, which is based on the characteristics of the organisation or the department and on the completed questionnaires, is to ensure that job analyst and job-holder have the same picture of the job. If the employee makes the description of his job himself, the characteristics of both the organisation and his department provide useful information on the interrelationships between department and jobs. This may lead to a proper view on the boundaries of responsibilities and competence.

Job description

The job description needs to comply with the demands of uniformity. The emphasis is on a proper representation of most of the essential characteristics of the job, the level of the job (not through a description of the required education and training), the importance of the activities for the organisation and the results the job is aiming for.

Approval of the job description

Obtaining approval is in essence reaching agreement between the employee and his immediate superior on whether the description defines the content of the job properly. It is essential that the department manager bears ultimate responsibility, because the set up of his department is closely related to the responsibility of the boss for realising the objectives and achieving the ultimate results. On the other hand the function-holder is the one who is confronted with the daily problems in the work assigned to him. Ultimately this part of the procedure should result in the holder of the job and the immediate superior both signing the final job description. One observation needs to be made. In a substantial number of cases the immediate boss tends to agree with the job description after having assured himself that it *does not contain any errors or omissions*. The holder of the job is usually *not* asked whether in his opinion the job description provides a correct and complete picture of the job and its responsibilities and competence. It is therefore recommended that the job description is also signed by the next higher superior. This manager is also the person who decides if the holder of the job and his boss cannot reach agreement on the job description.

Job analysis and job evaluation

The analysis and evaluation of the job are carried out by the person who has been appointed, resulting in an overall score and a classification in a grade.

Procedure for appeals

According to the rules that have been established, an appeal can be made against both the job description and the job grade. The appeal may be put before an external or an internal official. An internal appeal will usually follow a course as described in Appendix 3 of the book. However, it is perfectly possible that on the basis of the provisions of the collective agreement, individual employees will involve experts of the trade union. A joint committee may then consider the appeal on condition that both parties agree to accept the decision of the committee. The factual arrangement may vary in different industries.

In addition, the procedures need to be explained to the employees. What is the purpose of different steps? Who can be consulted if the employee does not agree with the course of action? The procedure also requires the establishment of committees, rules and regulations for these committees, forms, etc. Proper education and communication here is indispensable. The next section gives some guidelines and examples.

2.4 COMMUNICATION

Adequate communication is therefore of great importance to the success of job evaluation projects (see Figure 2.4). The ultimate goal is to ensure that employees have a proper understanding of the whole process. Information may be provided in personal meetings, or through a brochure containing the following elements:

- an explanation on why job evaluations are carried out (objectives);
- a short discussion of the methods of job evaluation that will be used;
- instructions on how to make a job description;
- model job descriptions;
- an explanation on how the system of job evaluation will be implemented (see Appendices 1 and 2 in which some accompanying forms have been included);
- a description of the appeal procedure (see Appendix 3);
- rules and regulations for supervising committees (see Appendix 4).

Also included may be an additional questionnaire and, if possible, 'blind' evaluation charts from the job evaluation method to be used. Blind evaluation charts do not contain any figures for weighing jobs.

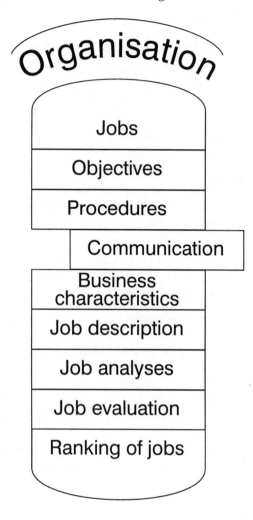

Figure 2.4 The process of job evaluation – communication

With these charts the employee is not able to evaluate his own job, but has some idea on what basis his job will be evaluated. Using blind charts as an illustration is usually an acceptable compromise if the owner of the method does not want to provide all details of the method.

The amount and content of the information should, of course, be attuned to the employees involved. General guidelines are inappropriate and useless. In most cases the owner of the system has sufficient documents on the basis of which an informative brochure can be put together.

This certainly does not complete the communication process. Experience teaches us that only a small proportion of the employees involved will read the brochure, at least before their own evaluation project starts. Thus it is important that the employees will be involved in the analyses as much as possible right from the start. The best results will be obtained through *oral* communication. However, this type of communication requires, on the part of the person who is in charge of this task, a profound knowledge of the method of job evaluation to be used. In addition, it should be realised that to many individuals job evaluation is a difficult subject. Another problem is how job evaluation can be made comprehensible to the different groups and levels of employees. It should be realised that job evaluation is not a science, but a practical technique. Moreover, the employees involved generally show only a limited willingness to really understand the job evaluation method. Usually they are only interested in the results of the investigation and analyses.

In the communication process, therefore, emphasis needs to be placed upon the various aspects of the way in which job evaluations are carried out. The focus therefore should be primarily on the procedures and practices which must ensure that the analyses and evaluations are executed as carefully and as meticulously as possible, and at the same time are flexible enough to respond to the problems and queries of the individual employee during the process.

The subjects which the communication process needs to deal with include:

- procedures and practices;
- composition and objectives of the supervising committee;
- explanations of the questionnaire and its function for the job description;
- a broad outline of the job evaluation method;
- the way in which the results of a job evaluation are reflected in the individual salary.

Preferably the communication process should take place in small groups of employees, as in bigger groups the individual employee can only listen and has no opportunity for putting questions or being heard. If in these meetings overhead sheets are used, it may be a good idea to provide the participants with copies after the meeting.

The various groups that require training and communication include:

- personnel officers;
- management;
- (formal) representatives of the workforce and/or trade unions;
- employees and groups of employees involved;
- members of the supervising committees of the job evaluation project.

These groups and individuals need to be addressed at their own level, taking into account their role and contribution to the organisation and the process of job evaluation. Obviously the owner of the system will provide assistance, particularly concerning technical matters, but it should be realised that members of the personnel function know the organisation and the employees best. Good communications are only possible if the owner of the system and the personnel manager collaborate as one team.

Some groups may need training in using the method, depending on the degree to which they will be involved in applying the method of job evaluation. It is, therefore, recommended that the (official) representatives of the workforce and members of the supervising committees are given first-hand experience in evaluating jobs. In a later stage they will then be in a better position to perform their role in the job evaluation process.

This section on communication and training concludes the discussion of the preparation of the project. If the suggestions have been followed, all groups and individuals concerned should know the purpose of the project and the way in which its objectives will be achieved. The next step is to acquire a thorough understanding of the organisation as a whole and of the interrelationships of its departments and activities.

2.5 BUSINESS CHARACTERISTICS

In section 1.3 we discussed the role of job evaluation in personnel management. At that point we linked the *rationale* of the organisation to the *quality of working life* in it through the integrative model. In this section we will explain the relationship between *rationale* and the *design* of the organisation. The relationship between the quality of working life and design also has some important implications. A job that contributes to the quality of the working life of employees is shaped through the design of the organisation on condition that the *rationale* is not put at risk.

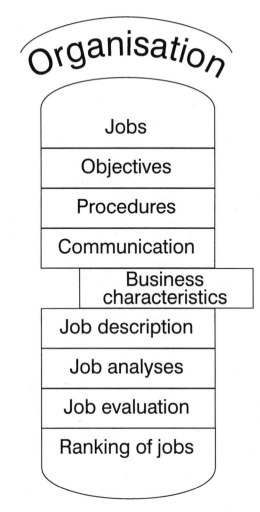

Figure 2.5 *The process of job evaluation – business characteristics*

If an attractive and pleasant job is inefficient and ineffective, it may endanger the rationale of the organisation and thus its entire existence. A job which is inhuman or impossible to perform, and in which all attention is concentrated on its effectiveness and efficiency, is also a risk to the survival of the organisation.

The description of the business characteristics (see Figure 2.5), and the job descriptions based on it, should thus reflect all conditions on its existence in a balanced way. Whereas the rationale of the organisation (its products, services, markets, targets, etc) is explicitly identified as part of the business characteristics, its purpose, objectives, tasks, processes and structures, which are the starting point of personnel management, are implicitly included.

Based on the conditions of the organisation, we focus on the quality of working life. All other applications of job description are less relevant to our purpose and will therefore not be discussed. Our subject is restricted to the job and the financial rewards for the efforts to achieve its objectives. The design, though, is a starting point for the justification of the job and its remuneration. It is thus very important to identify and record the design of the organisation. This is done by means of two closely related descriptions: of the business characteristics and of the characteristics of the department.

Usually organisations are divided into departments/activities, which then are split up into functions. The purpose is to form units, each in their own distinctive way and fashion contributing to the objectives of the organisation. This implies that they are able to operate independently from each other and that they are co-ordinated to optimise their activities. Job evaluation is an excellent instrument with which to analyse and record these relationships, not so much according to their task, but to their responsibilities/accountablities.

An organisation usually has a complex structure. If jobs are described separately from each other, we may lose sight of their mutual dependence. Thus it is useful to identify systematically the characteristics of the organisation, which we will refer to as the business characteristics and which visualise these interrelationships.

A survey of the business characteristics includes information on:

- the present position of the organisation;
- the purpose of the organisation;
- the direction of the organisation.

This overview may also act as the basis of a survey of the characteristics of a specific department.

The survey of business characteristics, which should be made independent of the particular methods of job evaluation to be used, consists of the following elements:

History

A short paragraph on the strategically important developments in the history of the organisation.

Main activities

A description of the distinguishing activities of the organisation. What is the main purpose of the organisation and what are the long-term objectives of its activities?

Organisational structure

The structure of the organisation will be represented through an organisation diagram or chart (Figure 2.2) which includes the functional areas. In addition, the number of employees of each function is indicated (personnel plan). Particulars of the organisation are provided separately. To be clear, the chart should not be too detailed and elaborate. At the end a short description of the rationale of each functional area is included, indicating its main responsibilities, the interrelationships between various areas and their contribution to achieving the objectives of the organisation.

Key products and markets

An outline is included of the key products/services which result from the main activities and with which the customers are being served. It also contains some general information on the product lines, the technology applied, key trends, present and future markets and market shares, prospective customers, expected or anticipated growth rates, the industry, competitors and other environmental forces.

Production process

A systematic overview/description is included which provides some details of the main activities. The activities are divided into sub-activities and a short description is given of the flows of information and of products/goods.

Strategic issues

The strategic issues/actions resulting from the purpose of the organisation are shown in the outline. This information may be a translation or a summary of the strategic plan.

Budget

This summary provides important figures from the budget of the organisation and its departments. These figures concern the present situation and the long term.

In Appendix 6 a sample is provided of a survey of the business characteristics of a publishing firm, a subsidiary of a large publishing group. In section 2.6 the job of Head of Personnel and Organisation within this firm is described in some detail.

The strategy charts (Figure A.6.4 in Appendix 6), which are also called Strengths, Weaknesses, Opportunities, Threats Analysis (SWOT), give a clear picture of the problems with which the organisation is confronted.

The survey of the business characteristics in this example assumes that all basic information has to be brought together to obtain one general overview on the design of the organisation, which is essential for identifying or investigating the rationale of the organisation. It provides insight into the interrelationships of the organisation as the basis from which the individual jobs can be derived.

As the company grows and becomes more complex there will be a need to elaborate the earlier established objectives of departments into departmental characteristics. A survey of the business characteristics, as described above, can be seen as the basic document of the Personnel and Organisation Department, which then can be used for the development of a personnel policy and a manpower plan. The approach for describing and surveying the organisation will also be useful as a background for job descriptions.

The publishing firm, Fiction, is part of a larger group, which consists of several subsidiaries located within one country. Such a company would prefer to co-ordinate a number of activities from its headquarters. The first reason is simply to comply with the legal obligations concerning the publication of its financial statements, tax issues and the like. In this area the Personnel and Organisation department will also benefit from a certain degree of co-ordination in the area of terms of employment and collective labour agreements, as it is very impractical to have different parts of an organisation negotiate independently with trade unions on these issues. In addition, such a lack of co-ordination would obstruct the flow of employees to other, superior positions. Also their capabilities would be wasted and they would feel restricted in their personal and professional development. For a further treatment of these subjects we refer to the substantial number of books and articles available. The Head of Personnel and Organisation of the publishing firm Fiction is required to apply the centrally formulated rules concerning its personnel policy and in particular its policy for the term of employment. Thus there exists a functional relationship between the job of Head of Personnel of the group and the job with the similar title within Fiction. This information will be used when we discuss the job description, analysis and evaluation.

In general the description of a department will differ from the business characteristics as its use is more restricted. It includes the following elements:

Objective

This is a short paragraph on the 'rationale' of the department, ie what the contribution of this department is to the final product or the end result of the organisation.

Organisation

An organisation chart of the department, linked to the chart of the organisation included in the survey of the business characteristics. It includes each function within the department and gives the number of employees working in each function.

Activities

Referring to the objectives of the department, a survey is presented on the key activities and performances of the department.

Key figures

In addition to the budget of the department, relevant quantitative data on the department may be provided.

Specific information

It is important that the survey of the business characteristics and the description of the department are both signed by their respective heads. These documents constitute a clear basis for the interviews to be held and prevent irrelevant discussion and disputes on delegating authority and responsibilities. A good job evaluation project starts with a preliminary discussion with management which should confirm the validity of both the survey of the business characteristics and the descriptions of the department(s).

The extent to which both documents on characteristics are used depends mainly on the complexity and size of the organisation. In a smaller organisation it will be sufficient to draw up a comprehensive survey of the business characteristics for the entire organisation, providing a clear picture of the assumptions, principles and objectives of its various units. In addition to this, a somewhat larger organisation may wish to have a short profile of the various departments. These profiles delineate the responsibilities and, if needed, they provide more details of each functional area in the form of a survey of the characteristics of departments. In very large, complex organisations the level of detail of the summaries of the organisation, as a whole and of its parts, may be such that comparisons between business and departmental characteristics can be made, which may be useful or indeed necessary. It is essential that:

> The description of the organisation starts from the rationale of the organisation and then makes clear how the organisation is designed and structured. It provides a framework in which to view jobs in this organisation within their mutual relationships.

Information obtained from interviews must never be in conflict or contradict the description of the organisation as provided by the survey of business characteristics. The job description, which we will discuss in the next section, is inseparably linked to the business characteristics. This has the additional advantage that information from the business or department characteristics need not be included in the job description itself. In this way it will be shorter and requires less maintenance.

2.6 THE JOB DESCRIPTION

The job description is the basis and starting point of the job evaluation process (see Figure 2.6). The importance of a proper job description cannot be stressed too much. There must not be any misunderstanding on the contents of the job description between the employee concerned, his immediate superior and the persons who carried out the survey and the job evaluation.

As their names imply, systems for job evaluation are directed at *jobs* or positions, not at *persons*. This crucial point must be decisive in describing a job.

In drawing up a job description, the way in which the holder of a job performs will not be assessed or discussed. Only elements of a job, which should be performed following the objectives of the organisation, are relevant to the analysis. The way in which an individual operates frequently has implications for the quality and quantity of

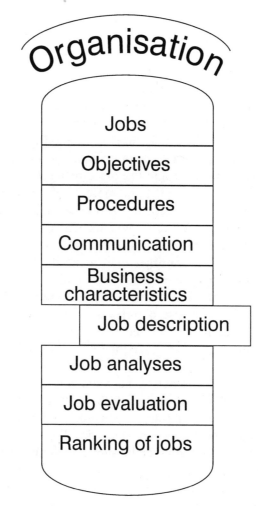

Figure 2.6 *The process of job evaluation – the job description*

the work carried out, but also influences the environment in which the holder of the job has performed his duties.

The quality and quantity of the work done and the extent of the tasks (which the holder of the job may have increased or decreased on his own initiative) will not be taken into consideration in describing that job. They are only taken into account when assessing the performance of the individual within the context of the personnel evaluation or merit rating.

A question frequently asked is 'Which situation is being described?' Will the factual situation be the basis, or the desired or normative situation? If the factual situation is described the result is a job description which is clear to the holder of the job. If the purpose of the description process is to arrive at a standard for the job, it must be made clear that without an assessment of the way in which the job is performed and without a specific training or education, the job requirements cannot be met. A factual description of the job will require more maintenance than a standard job description, because small changes in the job may necessitate modifying the description. In the case of a standard description an adaptation is only necessary if the organisation itself and the place of the job in it are changed. Thus an organisation needs to be more careful with its standardised job descriptions. Employees need to be evaluated on the extent to which they meet the job requirements. The evaluation process may result in targeted training and education to achieve the desired performance level. Sometimes one of the results of the evaluation will be a transfer to another job. Without an evaluation of the performance and the training level of the individual, the standard job description will soon lose its relevance to the organisation and the employees concerned. It will be clear that a standard approach will be difficult if the purpose of the job evaluation process is formulated too narrowly.

Monitoring the distinction between job and job-holder should mainly be a task of the immediate boss of the job-holder. The job-holder and his boss are jointly responsible for a correct representation of tasks, competences and responsibilities. For this reason is it recommended that the job evaluation be signed by both the superior and the job-holder(s).

This does not mean that the holder of the job can refuse to carry out tasks that have not been included in the job description, or derive rights or privileges from it, unless this is clearly stated

---

The job description is in most cases not an exhaustive rendering of all that is expected of the holder of the job. It includes those elements that are essential for a proper evaluation of the job level.

Before discussing the job description in more detail, it is useful to refer back to the business characteristics as this is the basis for the existence of the job. Also the integrative model of the organisation should be kept in mind.

The layout of the job description differs depending on the holder of the job. However, two elements are always included:

- the purpose of the job; and
- its place within the organisation.

These elements are discussed first, before entering into the other (varying) elements of a job description.

Purpose of the job

To describe the purpose of a function in a precise and relevant way is a very difficult task indeed. One easily tends to make the description too elaborate or divide it into several parts. The word 'objective' is to be taken as: *the object which the job is aimed at, which a job-holder tries to achieve, to realise.'*

In order to arrive at a proper description of the objective, one has to have a clear picture of the purpose and objectives of the organisation or the part of the organisation to which the job belongs. The job cannot be an independent, stand-alone unit, its existence ultimately being derived from the objectives of the organisation. This means that a job should be indispensable for achieving one or more objectives of the organisation. Another principle is that the objective of the job as laid down in the job description should fit in the hierarchy. This requires that the objective of the job should be linked logically to the stated objective of the next higher job.

By describing the objective of a job, its rationale, or the reason for its existence, is recorded. In a few words its purpose is laid down concisely. This is not the same as a short description or survey of the job.

An example of the description of the job objective of a director of an administrative and financial staff department could be:

> To provide financial information and reports which allow the Board and the Managing Director to plan, manage and control the financial performances and results of the company

An example of a description of the objective of the job of construction engineer is:

> To ensure the sound construction, correct measurements and proper finishing of buildings under construction

An example of the description of the objective of the job of the mail room is:

> To provide for the efficient distribution, processing, coding, managing and filing of documents and reception of documents, in order to manage the internal flow and preservation of documents

Take care that the description of the objective is always short and concise.

Place in the organisation

The description of the place of a job in the organisation must make clear how the job fits in and is related to the organisation as a whole. This requires at least insight into the immediate environment of the job. Who is the immediate superior? Which employees report to the same superior (managerial scope of the superior position or its span of control)? Are there any jobs reporting to the position described? If so, which jobs (managerial scope of the job)? Some job evaluation systems only require a statement on who is the immediate superior and how many subordinates report to that job. In general, this information is insufficient to form a proper picture of the situation. The best way to delineate the place of a job in the organisation is to draw an organisation chart (see Figure 2.7).

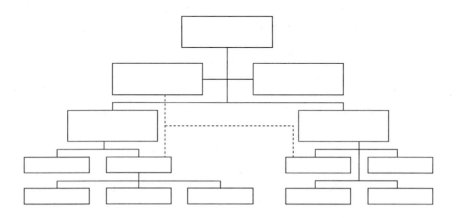

Figure 2.7:   *The organisation chart, showing hierarchical and functional relationships.*

The hierarchical relationships are represented by a c
tional or professional relationships by a dotted lin
information hardly ever makes the chart easier to rea
include additional information in the (survey of the) l
teristics.

This concludes the discussion of the place of a job in the organisation. We now proceed to the differences in job description of the various systems. Note that the format of a description will not be determined by the consultancy firm which performs the job evaluation project. To a large extent format and content should be established by the organisation itself. The following example illustrates job descriptions that Hay uses as a standard. Hay and other consultancy firms are very flexible and will take into account any special wishes and needs of the organisation. Sometimes a distinction is made between the type of job descriptions for managerial or higher staff positions on the one hand and for operational, task-oriented jobs on the other.

The Hay job description

Relevant quantitative information

The data on a job consist of quantified information that expresses the differences with comparable jobs. They provide insight into the variables that are controlled by the job. The Hay method does not deal with delineation risks but is directed at assessing the scope of the activities of the job-holder, ie the extent of the area directly or indirectly under his control and influence. Depending upon the type of job this scope may be expressed in monetary terms, but also in numbers.

- The scope of a sales job will be specified in terms of sales, cost budget and value added.
- The extent of a job in the HRM department may be expressed through the total amount of wages, the training budget and the number of employees.
- For a buyer in the purchasing department the scope of his job may be indicated by the total value of the goods and services bought and the value of the inventory.

All amounts are annualised. It may be useful not only to include the figures for the current year but also for the next planning period. This may indicate whether the job has stabilised or is still growing.

Principal accountabilities

This is, in effect, the most difficult part of making a job description. The Hay method concentrates on the relative importance of a job for achieving (sub-) objectives of the company. In this approach the emphasis is on the end results that are expected of that job. These end results are called accountabilities. It does not matter much how these end results are achieved, but rather of what they consist. It is important that the number of accountabilities remains limited. If not, duplication may occur and the accountabilities turn out to be a summary description of tasks and responsibilities. Special attention should be paid to the distinction between an accountability and a task. What delineates a job? Not its execution, but the results of the efforts.

To illustrate this difference, we give an example of the tasks and accountabilities of the job of an estate agent (see Figure 2.8).

A well-formulated accountability provides more and better information than a summary of the separate tasks.

The description of accountabilities consists of three elements:

1. *What?* What action(s) are required or need to be taken?
2. *Where?* In which accountability areas should (these) actions be taken?
3. *What for?* Which results should be achieved by these actions?

For each accountability a description will be made of its key activities. This direct link between key activities and accountabilities gives a concise representation of the job, without any duplication.

Appendix 7 provides by way of an example the job description of a (departmental) Secretary according to the Hay method. To give an impression of the difference between a lower and a higher job, Appendix 8 contains the job description of the Head of the Personnel Department of a publishing company.

2.7 ANALYSING A JOB

In analysing a job we determine whether the characteristics or requirements of the proposed method are applicable to the job and if so, to what extent (see Figure 2.9). For example, which level of knowledge (as defined by the method under consideration) is required to perform the job? Note that the individual competences of the job-holder do not play any role. The best preparation for

Tasks

- Placing of advertisement for property for sale and welcoming potential buyers
- Upon request, surveying property and drafting survey reports
- Negotiating on the price of the property on behalf of the client
- Taking care of the administrative settlement of transactions

Accountabilities

- Ensuring that through an appropriate advertising campaign sufficient interest is raised
- Influencing potential buyers of the property in such a way that the probability of arriving at a sale is maximised
- Negotiating on the price within the limits set by the client in order to achieve a result that is acceptable to the client

Tasks to be accomplished

within the context of

Key activities on a particular area

aimed at achieving

The expected end results

Tasks are:
activities that must be performed within the job

Activities are:
actions that, as a consequence of a job, need to be in order to produce the expected end results

Performance areas:
describe the main activities that make it possible to achieve the end results as well as the immediate impact on these end results

Figure 2.8   *Accountability areas versus tasks*

analysing a job is to describe the degree in which a specific characteristic or requirement must be satisfied in order to perform the job adequately.

The Hay Guide Chart and Profile Method – the Hay method – takes a somewhat different approach, which we will illustrate through the example of the analysis of the job of personal secretary.

In this method, the Hay Guide Chart and Profile Method, the requirement or characteristic 'know-how' of a job is defined as follows:

> Know-how is the sum of every kind of knowledge, skill and experience however acquired, needed for standard acceptable job performance.

The analysis of the job of personal secretary, according to the Hay method, results in the following statements.

A personal secretary performs all standard secretarial tasks for one or more persons who usually operate at the middle management level. She or he performs standard administrative activities in connection with these secretarial tasks.

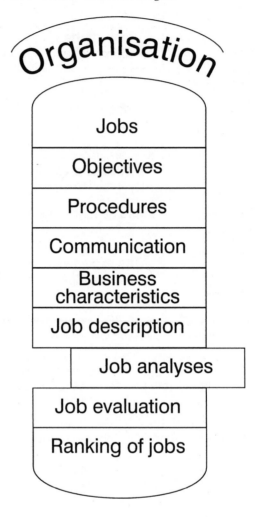

Figure 2.9 *The process of job evaluation – analysing a job.*

The job requires a sound independent judgement and a good knowledge of the way in which the superior(s) work(s). In addition, substantial experience as a secretary is necessary. Besides proficiency in English, some knowledge of a foreign language (German/French) is required.

The characteristics of jobs and their various factors or aspects according to the Hay method can be structured in the way which is illustrated in Table 2.1.

Characteristic	Factor
Know-how	Technical know-how Breadth of management know-how Human relations skills
Problem solving	Thinking environment – freedom to think Thinking challenge
Accountability	Freedom to act Magnitude Impact

Table 2.1 *Characteristics and factors/aspects of the Hay Guide Chart and Profile method.*

As is evident from this table the interrelationships between these characteristics are relatively simple. If more characteristics are used in analysing a job, more attention needs to be paid to the interrelationships of the various characteristics.

The choice of characteristics of jobs follows from the following reasoning:

- the results for which the job is held *accountable* ⟶ output
- require an amount of *know-how* ⟶ input
  and
- the processing of the know-how required for the job through the conscious thinking process or
  problem solving ⟶ throughput or processing

in order to achieve the expected *end results*.

This process is visualised in Figure 2.10.

Though the Hay method does not use a weighing factor for each characteristic, the relationship between the aspects is determined by the quantified comparisons ('numbering pattern') on the evaluation charts ('Guide Charts'). The quantified comparisons or ratios are based on the concept of the 'just noticeable difference' which is derived from Weber's Law. The *just noticeable difference* is the smallest difference which a person can observe in the degrees in which a characteristic is required for jobs. Applied to weighing job

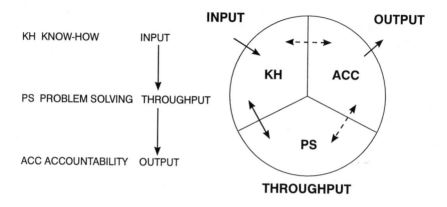

Figure 2.10: *Relationships between characteristics of the Hay Guide charts.*

requirements or characteristics, the following 'scores' are given to the difference in a characteristic required for two comparable jobs:

- a *just noticeable difference*; the jobs are considered to be *one step* apart;
- a *clearly noticeable difference*; the jobs are considered to be *two steps* apart;
- a *quite evident difference*; for this characteristic the jobs are *three steps or more* apart.

In the Hay method a distance of one step is considered to be equivalent to a difference of 15 per cent. This 15 per cent difference constitutes the basis of the 'numbering pattern' of quantitative comparisons in the evaluation charts.

In addition to the *characteristics* of jobs, the Hay method uses the so-called job profile. This is a practical judgement of the nature of the job in relation to the objectives and end results to be achieved in the job. The job profile is used:

- to check whether the evaluation is correct;
- to monitor the degree of the involvement of the job in (primary) processes of the business;
- as an instrument for judging the relationships and ratios in jobs and levels of the required characteristics which have been found in the evaluation process.

The method uses two types of profiles; the short profile and the long one.

The short profile represents the ratio between problem solving (PS) and the extent of the accountability (ACC) as measured in the steps concept of Hay. If the score for the extent of the accountability (ACC) is higher than that for problem solving (PS), the job is said to have an A-profile. In the opposite case the resulting profile is called a P-profile. If the scores for both characteristics are equal, the profile is called an L-profile (Level). As is illustrated in Figure 2.11 the range of feasible profiles is A1, A2, A3, A4, L, P1, P2, P3 and P4. The figures 1, 2, 3 and 4 indicate the difference between the scores for ACC and PS, expressed in steps of 15 per cent.

A-profiles

In the A-profile the emphasis is on the extent of the accountability. Distinctive A-profiles (A4 and A3) indicate in general that the jobs are action-oriented and have a strong influence on the end results to be achieved. Managerial jobs tend to have an A3 or A4 profile. Operational jobs and jobs supervising the various primary processes of the firm also have A-profiles.

A2-profiles can be found for managerial jobs in which problem solving is a major component. Examples are jobs in charge of a staff department or a supporting function (to line management). A1-profiles occur mainly in supporting and advisory functions and in operational jobs, like secretaries and administrative assistants.

P-profiles

The emphasis of P-profiles is on dealing with and solving problems, while the extent of the accountability is less prominent. Solitary, non-managerial jobs in Research and Development or in engineering are usually of a nature that matches a P-profile. P4-profiles can be found for jobs that are entirely in the field of basic research. Jobs that are in charge of small research units may also show a P-profile.

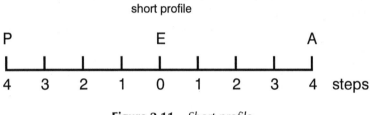

Figure 2.11 *Short profile*

L-profiles

For jobs with an L-profile the numbers of steps for the characteristics 'extent of the accountability' and 'problem solving' are equal. Jobs with a P1-profile or an A1-profile differ only a little from the L-profile. Many supporting jobs, such as strictly staff positions and managerial jobs which concentrate on problem-solving activities, show these profiles.

In determining the 'long profile' or the percentage profile, the job is viewed in its entirety in order to examine the interrelationships between the three characteristics. The value of each characteristic is expressed as a percentage of the total score possible. For example:

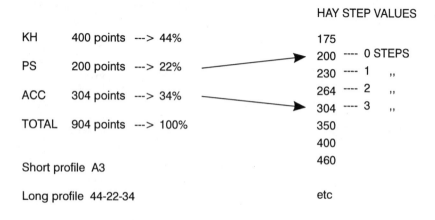

HAY STEP VALUES

KH	400 points ---> 44%	175
		200 ---- 0 STEPS
PS	200 points ---> 22%	230 ---- 1 ,,
		264 ---- 2 ,,
ACC	304 points ---> 34%	304 ---- 3 ,,
		350
TOTAL	904 points ---> 100%	400
		460

Short profile A3

Long profile 44-22-34   etc

Note on the short profile

The difference between ACC and PS amounts to three steps, while ACC has the highest score. Thus the job has an A3-profile.

Note on the long profile

Equate the total score of 904 to 100 per cent. Then the share of know-how (KH) of 400 points equals: (400/904) x 100 = 44 per cent. Similarly we find for the PS share 22 per cent and for ACC 34 per cent.

A more specialised job will show a higher percentage KH, while the percentage AC decreases as the job is located lower down the hierarchy. The ratios within the short and the long profile are independent of the score. In Figure 2.12 a comparison is made between the above example and another job with a lower score, both of which have different profiles.

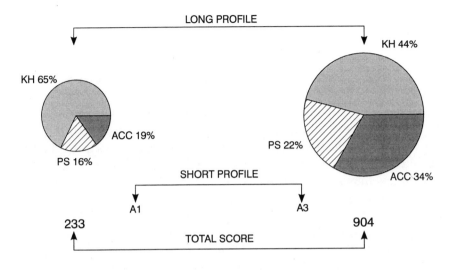

Figure 2.12 *Comparison of profiles versus total score*

For the composition of the profile several conclusions can be drawn.

- In the case of two subordinate jobs the higher job will also show a higher ACC score in the long profile. This score reflects that the higher job is 'more accountable for end results' than the lower job.
- As the job is located lower down the hierarchy, the percentage ACC decreases, whereas the percentage KH increases.
- The composition of the long profile indicates whether a job is a staff or line position. In the case of a line job the emphasis is on ACC, whereas for a staff job the KH percentage is relatively high.
- A manager at a higher level scores a higher percentage for PS and ACC and a lower percentage for KH than a manager at a lower level. The former is more like a generalist, whereas the latter is in general more like a specialist.
- In supporting and research jobs the emphasis is on KH and PS. The percentage score ACC will be lower in these jobs.
- The extent of the influence of supporting jobs on the decision-making process of line management (co-management) is reflected in the percentages for ACC of both types of jobs.
- Normally only specific ratios in the percentages for ACC of jobs within the hierarchy can be acted upon.

- In matrix organisations and in project management the percentages ACC will be closer to each other than between hierarchical levels in classical organisation structures.

After careful consideration some conclusions can be drawn from the results of job evaluations regarding the relationships and links between jobs. An experienced user (system-holder) will certainly be able to provide such insight. None of the methods discussed emphasises these applications for profiling and comparing jobs as explicitly as the Hay method does. The more detailed description of the Hay method is thus meant to demonstrate that the results of job evaluation may be useful tools for an organisation to analyse, characterise and correlate jobs.

The analyst is only able to make a proper analysis if he knows all characteristics of the method and their mutual relationships. Therefore after the example of the secretary this section has focused on the method of Hay. What information these methods have produced in this section must be in accordance with the motivation that will be provided by evaluating the knowledge required for this function. Next, after careful consideration of the definitions of the table entries, the correct entry for this job in the table 'know-how' can be determined.

2.8 EVALUATING A JOB

2.8.1 Construction and use of evaluation tables

Evaluating jobs consists of assigning scores to various job characteristics included in the method being used (see Figure 2.13). To determine the score of a particular characteristic the analyst needs to determine the applicable entry code to the evaluation table of the method. Most methods which use points have tables in the form of a matrix (see Table 2.2).

The table entries in this example have been coded by the letters a, b, c and d for the vertical columns and the numbers 1, 2 and 3 for the horizontal rows. If we choose the entry codes b and 2 in this table, we find a score of 25 points. Some job evaluation methods, such as the Hay method, do not allow a value to be chosen in between the values included in the table. Other methods do allow interpolations between the values provided. For both approaches some valid arguments can be given. If we take the latter approach, the following notations of scores can be determined:

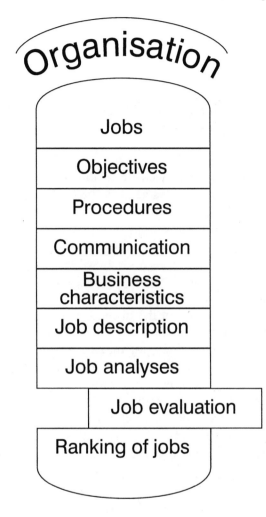

Figure 2.13 *The process of job evaluation – evaluating a job*

b/c 2	or	b + 2	score = 28
b/c 2	or	b + 2	score = 31
b/c 2/3	or	b + 2 +	score = 38
b/c 2/3	or	b + 3 –	score = 38

Note that these codings and numbers have been chosen arbitrarily, the point being to demonstrate the use of these types of tables.

Table X	1	2	3
a	10	15	20
b	20	25	30
c	30	35	40
d	40	45	50

Table 2.2: *Simplified matrix table*

It is important that clear rules are established on the way in which the notation of the table entries needs to be interpreted. This is not just a matter of co-ordination between job analysts. The notation also contains information for the personnel manager or head of the department, which he may need in explaining the evaluation results to the job-holders.

In the Hay method, assigning values included in the table is not allowed as this method is based on the so-called concept of steps. According to this concept the distance between successive values is defined as 'a just noticeable difference'. In view of this definition a value between steps does not make sense. Nevertheless the Hay method allows for smaller nuances and refinements when choosing the table entry, as is shown by the following examples. As in Table 2.2 the figures in these examples need not correspond with factual evaluation tables of both methods. We just want to demonstrate their construction. According to the Hay method we may have derived the following scores from Table 2.3:

Table X	1	2	3
A	5 10 15	10 15 20	15 20 25
B	15 20 25	20 25 30	25 30 35
C	25 30 35	30 35 40	35 40 45
D	35 40 45	40 45 50	45 50 55

Table 2.3 *A more extensive matrix table*

b 2	score 25	b + 2	score 30
b + 2 -	score 25	b 2 +	score 30
c 2 +	score 25	b - 2	score 20
b - 2 -	score 20*		
b + 2 +	score 30*		

* These scores make no sense as they produce the same result as, for instance, 'b – 2' and 'b + 2'.

In interpreting the tables and definitions of a particular job evaluation method, reference or benchmark jobs are indispensable. These benchmark jobs should therefore be seen as an integral part of that job evaluation method. A benchmark job has been described, evaluated and commented upon in such a way that complete agreement has been established between system-holder and other parties involved.

2.8.2 Evaluating jobs with the Hay method

As has been discussed above, the Hay method evaluates jobs on the basis of three characteristics or 'aspects'; know-how, problem solving and accountability. We start with the evaluation chart (which is called the 'Guide Chart') for the characteristic 'know-how'. This chart differentiates between three aspects or factors:

- technical know-how;
- breadth of management know-how;
- human relations skills.

For the definitions of the table entries of the 'know-how' chart we refer to Table 2.4.

When evaluating the job of Secretary according to the Hay method, we arrive at entry C for the specialised and technical know-how. This know-how concerns carrying out practical techniques, processes and procedures, such as taking shorthand notes of texts, typing activities by means of word-processing techniques, working on a personal computer, operating printers, typewriters and facsimile machines, filing and keeping the office diary. In this job, insight into the technical operating procedures and methods concerns the knowledge of and some insight into the (commercial) activities of the department.

From the definition under D, 'advanced vocational knowledge', it will be clear that in this job of Secretary no 'specialised, generally non-technical know-how' is required. Also the job does not entail

DEFINITION

Know-How is the sum of every kind of knowledge, skill and experience required for standard acceptance job performance. It is the fund of knowledge (however acquired) which is necessary for meeting

:: The requirement for Know-How in practical procedures, specialised techniques and professional disciplines.

:: The requirement for Know-How in integrating and harmonising the diverse elements involved in managerial situations. This Know-How may be exercised in an advisory capacity as well as executively. It involves combining to some degree the elements of planning, organising, directing, controlling and innovating and takes account of size, functional or organisational diversity, and time scale.

:: The requirement for Know-How in working with and through people (within or outside the organisation)

MEASURING KNOW-HOW:

Know-How has both breadth and depth. Thus a job may require some knowledge about a lot of things, or a lot of knowledge about a few things. The total Know-How is the sum of breadth and depth. This concept makes practical comparison and weighing of the total Know-How content of different jobs in terms of 'HOW MUCH KNOWLEDGE ABOUT HOW MANY THINGS'

••• HUMAN RELATIONS SKILLS

1. BASIC:
Ordinary courtesy and effectiveness in dealing with others is required

2. IMPORTANT:
Understanding, influencing, and communicating with people are important but not overriding considerations

3. CRITICAL:
Skills in influencing developing and/or motivating people are critical to the achievement of job objectives

HAY GUIDE CHART FOR EVALUATING
KNOW-HOW

••• HUMAN RELATIONS SKILLS

PRACTICAL PROCEDURES

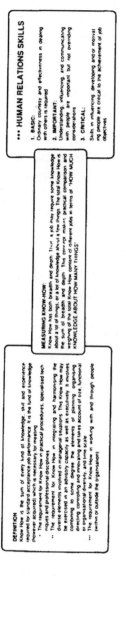

•• PLANNING, ORGANISING, CONTROLLING – BREADTH OF MANAGEMENT KNOW-HOW

	0. TASK			I. ACTIVITY			II. HOMOGENEOUS			III. HETEROGENEOUS			IV. (TOTAL)			
	Performance of a task (or tasks) highly specific as to objective and content and not involving the supervision of others			Performance of supervision of work which is specific as to objective and content with appropriate awareness of related activities			Internal integration of operations which are relatively homogeneous in nature and objective which involve external co-ordination with associated functions			Operational or conceptual integration of functions which are diverse in nature and in objective in an important management area, or central co-ordination of a strategic function						
	1.	2.	3.	1.	2.	3.	1.	2.	3.	1.	2.	3.	1.	2.	3.	
A PRIMARY Jobs requiring Secondary education only, plus some work indoctrination	38	43	50	50	57	66	66	76	87	87	100	115	115	132	152	**A**
	43	50	57	57	66	76	76	87	100	100	115	132	132	152	175	
	50	57	66	66	76	87	87	100	115	115	132	152	152	175	200	
B ELEMENTARY VOCATIONAL Jobs requiring familiarisation in uninvolved, standardised work routines and/or use of simple equipment and machines	50	57	66	66	76	87	87	100	115	115	132	152	152	175	200	**B**
	57	66	76	76	87	100	100	115	132	132	152	175	175	200	230	
	66	76	87	87	100	115	115	132	152	152	175	200	200	230	264	
C VOCATIONAL Jobs requiring procedural or systematic proficiency, which may involve facility in the use of specialised equipment	66	76	87	87	100	115	115	132	152	152	175	200	200	230	264	**C**
	76	87	100	100	115	132	132	152	175	175	200	230	230	264	304	
	87	100	115	115	132	152	152	175	200	200	230	264	264	304	350	

D ADVANCED VOCATIONAL. Jobs requiring some specialised (generally non-theoretical) skills gained by on the job experience or through part professional qualification	87	100	115	115	132	152	152	175	200	200	230	264	264	304	350
	100	115	132	132	152	175	175	200	230	230	264	304	304	350	400
	115	132	152	152	175	200	200	230	264	264	304	350	350	400	460
E BASIC PROFESSIONAL. Jobs requiring sufficiency in a technical scientific or specialised field based on an understanding of concepts and principles normally associated with a professional or academic qualification or gained through a detailed grasp of involved practices and procedures	115	132	152	152	175	200	200	230	264	264	304	350	350	400	460
	132	152	175	175	200	230	230	264	304	304	350	400	400	460	528
	152	175	200	200	230	264	264	304	350	350	400	460	460	528	608
F SEASONED PROFESSIONAL. Jobs requiring proficiency in a technical, scientific or specialised field gained through broad and deep experience built on concepts and principles or through wide exposure to complex practices and precedents	152	175	200	200	230	264	264	304	350	350	400	460	460	528	608
	175	200	230	230	264	304	304	350	400	400	460	528	528	608	700
	200	230	264	264	304	350	350	400	460	460	528	608	608	700	800
G PROFESSIONAL MASTERY. Jobs requiring determinative mastery of concepts, principles and practices gained through deep development in a highly specialised field or through comprehensive business experience	200	230	264	264	304	350	350	400	460	460	528	608	608	700	800
	230	264	304	304	350	400	400	460	528	528	608	700	700	800	920
	264	304	350	350	400	460	460	528	608	608	700	800	800	920	1056
H UNIQUE AUTHORITY. Jobs requiring outstanding knowledge and command of a profound discipline at a pre-eminent level	264	304	350	350	400	460	460	528	608	608	700	800	800	920	1056
	304	350	400	400	460	528	528	608	700	700	800	920	920	920	1056
	350	400	460	460	528	608	608	700	800	800	920	1056	1056	1216	1400

SPECIALISED TECHNIQUES

PROFESSIONAL DISCIPLINES

* DEPTH AND RANGE OF TECHNICAL KNOW-HOW

Table 2.4 Know-how chart

'specialised methods and processes that can be learned in a relatively short period of time' (entry C). After a preliminary choice of the table entry it is not only useful, but necessary, to read carefully the definitions just above and below that entry. Only then is it possible to make a proper selection and to establish the reasons for the choice.

The next characteristic is Managerial Skill. A personal secretary has a supporting role to the persons she works for. The job contains elements that concern the entire department. A series of issues for which personal initiative is expected bears upon the efficiency of the operations of the department. For these reasons Managerial Skills scores I instead of 0.

Finally the human resource skills need to be evaluated. These human resource skills refer to the degree in which others need to be influenced to obtain the expected results. The working relationship of a secretary with the department and its environment will generally be of an informative nature. Thus the choice will be 1.

The complete score for 'Knowledge' will thus be:

C I 1 score	115 points	
The total score is	177 points	A1-profile, 65–16–19

The mean value of the block has been chosen, because no further nuances have been used when selecting the entries. Comparison of this score and the score according to another method is not relevant, because of the difference in depth in which this characteristic is evaluated, in the sense that the Hay method goes further than most methods.

Next the job of Head of the Personnel Function will be evaluated on the basis of the Hay method.

In order to perform the job of Head of Personnel an individual needs professional education and training, because it is necessary to have insight into the theoretical fundamentals and relationships. Also a substantial degree of abstraction is needed to be able to understand and appreciate the processes in such an organisation. Designing and formulating a personnel policy or a social plan requires knowledge and expertise of an advanced professional level and a substantial number of years' experience in practice. The Head of Personnel has an important advisory and supporting role towards management and is involved in decision-making processes which are aimed at effectively and efficiently achieved short-term and long-term objectives. There is a demonstrable relationship between the quality of the functioning of the organisation (its rationale) and the advice of the Head of Personnel concerning the design of and the quality of working life in the organisation.

Which human resource skills are required, will, amongst other things, be determined by the expectation that the job-holder will convince and motivate others, frequently on the basis of non-rational arguments. In situations of conflict the job-holder must be able to mediate. These considerations result in the following evaluation:

EII 3 score	350 points		
The total score is	657 points	A2-profile	53–20–27

2.8.3 Evaluation procedure

An important element of the job evaluation method is the procedure and format of the evaluation process. When the evaluation is carried out by the system-holder or by someone under his direct supervision, it may lead to different results from those obtained when the organisation itself is responsible for the evaluation of jobs. Both approaches have advantages and drawbacks.

The former approach, referred to as the 'external approach', has been applied for a long time and is still preferred by many organisations. The latter approach is more in accordance with the views of the Hay Group and is referred to as the 'internal approach'. The organisation itself has to determine whichever approach it prefers. Choosing the external approach implies maximum objectivity, because the owner or holder of the system remains outside the organisation and will give the quality of the evaluation the highest priority. If the job evaluation is performed by management (Personnel Department), whether or not assisted by internal or external experts, maximum commitment concerning the results may be expected of the managers. This will consequently lead to a high degree of acceptance of the findings.

The internal approach is usually chosen to stress that the organisation accepts its responsibility for the evaluation process and its results.

2.8.4 Computerised job evaluation systems

Now we have discussed the technique of evaluating jobs in the previous four sections, it is appropriate to give a brief review of the latest developments in the field, in particular the use of the computer in evaluating jobs. Also, as can be expected in this area, there are differences in the views of system-holders. In addition, the available standard software is not limited to job evaluation as such; in a number of cases information on pay levels in the labour market is linked to the results of the evaluation process.

A first step when considering the implementation of a computerised system is making an assessment of the possibilities of the automated system in view of the objectives to be achieved with the aid of the system. The results of paired comparisons, and the subsequent classification of functions in job or salary groups, may inhibit the use of job evaluation, eg organisational analyses. The implementation of a computerised system may necessitate reconsidering accepted conditions and principles of job evaluation. It would not be wise to ignore such conditions in order to reap the undeniably considerable benefits of automated systems. One of the main advantages may be the consistency which is enforced by the application of these methods. By incorporating so-called validity checks, the input data will be checked and compared with predetermined standards. In addition, such checks signal if a particular answer to a question put by the system contradicts previous answers.

Computerised methods are an improvement as they save time and promote consistency in the application of job evaluation methods. However, they do not constitute a different approach to job evaluation.

An example of a computerised system that is linked to external pay information is the modular HayXpert system of Hay Management Consultants (see Figure 2.14). It is not the only method currently available that uses such a modular set-up.

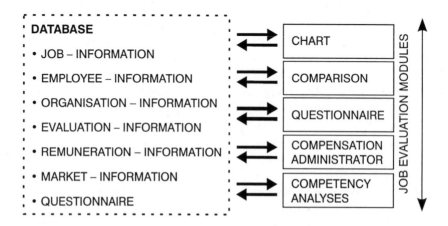

Figure 2.14: *Hay Xpert modules*

The HayXpert system is based on two elements: 'points' and 'reference' and is built on four modules for job evaluation; 'Chart', 'Comparison', and 'Questionnaire'.

Chart
This module contains a database for recording and consulting job information, previous evaluations and justification of the scores assigned, based on the Hay Guide Chart.

Comparison
Comparison is a factor-based approach to evaluating work (on the basis of three factors) within a given grade structure. As the scales are custom made to the organisation, no specific knowledge of the Hay method is required. The module can be used by management and provides substantial insight to the employees. 'Comparison' includes 'Chart' and can be developed for other job families as well.

Questionnaire
On the basis of a structured questionnaire the job level is established through an arithmetic model. 'Questionnaire' includes 'Chart' and allows for external comparisons through benchmark jobs in commercial organisations.

2.8.5 The job level matrix

Apart from point factor methods, which are sometimes called expert systems (in the case of Hay, Framework, EFP) another phenomenon gains increasing acceptance. A number of consultancy firms have introduced flexible methods for job evaluation in the market, called Job Family Systems. These provide a methodology that can be applied by a non-specialist manager. However, as in the point factor methods, the basis for establishing mutual relationships between the elements of a Job Family System is an expert system, as in point factor systems. In everyday use a Job Family System (JFS) does not require consulting point tables, but rather a matrix or grid. Because JFSs are built upon an expert system the facility to make external comparisons is ensured. This expert system is used to evaluate the series of benchmark jobs which need to be well established, clearly described and easily recognisable throughout the organisation. Preferably they are not linked to a specific individual and are not likely to be changed substantially in the foreseeable future. These requirements of benchmark jobs provide a sound basis for the JFS and allow for external comparisons.

The JFS methodology has two entries for classifying jobs: the combinations of different types of jobs, or job families (rows) and the number of job levels (columns). (See Table 2.5.) As previously stated the JFS is developed starting from an expert system. This describes and values the benchmark jobs (*c.* 25 per cent of the total job base). Very short descriptions of these jobs – subdivided according to job family – are included in the JFS as references for classifying the other jobs. For determining the level of a job, so-called level indicators have been established. These level indicators, apply formulated, summarised common characteristics of jobs within the same job group or 'grade'. In this way the difference between job levels can be clearly established. In fact the JFS is an elaboration and extension of the construction of so-called job series. A job series contains successive levels of the same job, in which each level represents a job grade. For instance, the job family consists of:

Departmental secretary	Grade 4
Secretary	Grade 5
PA/secretary to the Managing Director	Grade 6

For each of these jobs standardised job descriptions have been made, which clearly establish the core of a job. The degree in which the employee meets the specified job determines into which job family he is classified.

Tables 2.5 and 2.6 give examples of differently structured job level matrices. In conjunction with the given level indicator Table 2.5 provides a sample description of the respective levels of the activities. Other jobs from the same job family can be classified by comparing them with the sample descriptions, for example:

> The family group 'sales' gives at level 5 a description of the type of activities that match the description of the level indicator in the heading of the table. Other sales jobs can be compared with these and accordingly classified at the same, higher or a lower level

While Table 2.5 provides general descriptions as level indicators, Table 2.6 describes the various job levels within the job family Personnel. The precise set-up and contents of a job family system (JFS) depends upon the specific needs of the organisation.

When classifying the job of Head of Personnel the description of the job matches level 8.

Table 2.5: *Example of a Job Family System*

Level	4	5	6
Level indicator	Performs technical or specialist activities according to guidelines and is directly supervised. Has possibly operational responsibility for some employees carrying out routine operations	Performs technical or specialist activities comprising co-ordinating, preparatory and operational elements. Has possibly operational responsibility for some operational technical employees.	Performs specialist operational activities according to guidelines and with a large degree of autonomy. Has possible operational responsibility for some technical employees.
Sample description **Sales**		Visits (prospective) customers, closes transactions for the sales of books according to guidelines	
Sample description **Automation**	Records, co-ordinates and answers where possible questions from internal and external users. Manages the registration system of the project, supports the testing of the system		Plans the activities of the computer centre. Tests new applications, implements new methods. Keeps the departmental documentation up to date
Sample description **Finance and Accounting**		Performs the accounting of some products, checks the billing, the tapes for the collection of debts and payments. Reconciles the sub-accounting and the general ledger and prepares the internal reports.	Is in charge of the accounting of the internal receivables and payables. Presses for outstanding payments. Provides management information. Supervises some employees.

As when using expert systems, some conditions must be met before a job level matrix can be applied. These conditions concern the issue as to whether or not it is wise to implement a JFS at a particular moment. Similar to the considerations when introducing automated systems, the question arises to what extent the job level matrix contributes to achieving the original objectives of the job evaluation

Table 2.6 *Example of a Job Family System*

Level	4	5	6	8
Core Job	Head of Personnel Administration	Sector Personnel Manager	Head of Training and Development	Chief Personnel Officer
Level indicator	Advises on complex problems. Co-operates to some extent with other departments and disciplines. Has possibly operational responsibilities for (sub-) projects or for managing some employees.	Prepares personnel policy within designated projects and fields. Has possibly functional and operational responsibilities for more complex (sub-) projects or is in charge of some employees.	Prepares policy proposals in a specialist field and is professionally responsible for content and results. Has possibly functional responsibilities for complex (sub-) projects or is in charge of some employees.	Advises on policy at company level on the basis of a profound professional expertise and has final responsibility concerning complex issues and relationships within the context of the company policy or strategy. The activities are generally of a rather innovative and creative nature. Is possibly in charge of a department
Sample description	Is in charge of the department of personnel information and salary administration. Is in charge of preparing management information. Carries out some research in this field	Contributes to the development of social policy. Implements social policy within a section (personnel planning, recruitment, selection, collective conditions and termination). Advises and intermediates in case of labour conflicts. Is in charge of a team of employees.	Formulates the training and development policy of the organisation. Prepares training and development plans, develops methodologies and didactics. Is in charge of a team of internal training specialists.	Supervises advisory activities in the field of organisational change, conditions and terms of employment, job evaluation, training and development, company welfare, personnel management, etc. Prepares policy on social and organisational issues for the entire company. Manages and coaches change processes with a large impact on the organisation

project. Is it exclusively intended for remuneration purposes or will job evaluation be used for wider purposes?

The role of the Personnel Function in applying JFS differs from the one in expert systems and is in this case more that of a guardian of the system and procedures and of a coach than that of a department that carries out the evaluations or passes on the results. The first condition is that the Personnel Function is sufficiently trusted in the organisation to be able to adjust and manage the process. Also, it must be able to intervene if procedures are not or insufficiently followed and if adjustments or modifications of the JFS are necessary (maintenance). In addition, the Personnel Function must also take action if the operational process of classifying jobs on the basis of exchanges of views and of communicating the classification results to the employees is hampered or obstructed.

The second condition is that the Personnel Function possesses the professional skills required to perform its (new) role. The manager in charge should be of sufficient professional integrity to coach and support the process independently. This implies that the personnel officer can only have an advisory role in the evaluation committee. The Personnel Function should keep its distance to preserve an independent position from which it can be facilitator and coach and to participate in a committee for appeal.

The third condition is the quality of the management of the organisation. As has been pointed out before, JFS is carried out by management. Thus it should meet certain requirements. Not only must it be willing to carry out this task, it must also possess the necessary competences. These requirements concern mainly communication skills, because in JFS the management will have to communicate the results of the classification process in grades to the employees.

Finally, a summary of the implementation process of a JFS is given. This process consists of the following eight stages:

- education/communication;
- choice of core jobs and selection of job families;
- description and weighing of core jobs;
- testing the ranking of jobs and possibly weighing these rankings;
- establishing job families' structure;
- job matrix, classification and appeal procedures, and appointing and setting up a classification committee;
- classifying jobs;
- communicating the results.

A major advantage of JFS is that it provides insight into employees across job families and specialisations, because it gives a picture of the requirements and requirement levels of various jobs. How do you compare a job in the accounting department with a job in maintenance? As is the case with the job series discussed earlier, the JFS can be combined perfectly with flexible remuneration systems. We will discuss this in more detail in Part II. Finally, a widely accepted and consistent evaluation methodology provides the essential link between the JFS and the pay system.

2.9 RANKING OF JOBS

From a technical standpoint the weighing of jobs is the final step in the job evaluation process, provided all parties involved agree that the ranking correctly represents the relationships within the organisation. Only then can it be assumed that a basis has been established for developing a remuneration policy.

After careful consideration of the ranking list and in particular of the clusters of jobs in that list, it may appear that the position of some jobs does not seem logical (see Figure 2.15). In such cases it is recommended that the evaluation of that job is thoroughly checked and compared with jobs directly surrounding it ('cluster'). After these final checks and possible adjustments have been made, the ranking is ready for use.

After describing some basic concepts of salary structures sections 4.5 and 4.6 will discuss the ranking list as the starting point of the design of an 'own' salary structure. For an example of such a ranking list of jobs see Table 2.7.

Table 2.7   *Rank order of jobs*

Job evaluation points	Jobs
45	Cleaner
51	Delivery man
63	Driver
68	Typist
70	Receptionist
85	Departmental secretary
89	Receptionist/exchange operator
105	Computer operator
121	Head of post room
136	Secretary
148	Calculator/cost accountant
159	Programmer
165	Wage accountant/personnel administrator
193	Head of accounting
201	Marketing assistant
203	Sales representative
235	Systems manager
etc.	etc.

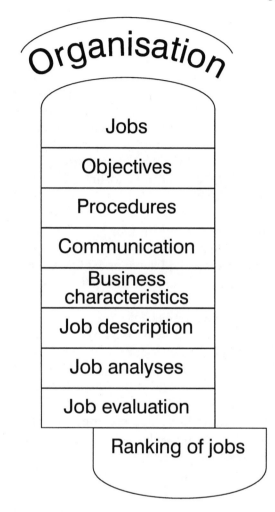

Figure 2.15 *The process of job evaluation – ranking of jobs*

2.10 CHECKLIST FOR JOB EVALUATION

At the end of this chapter we provide a checklist as a tool for making choices.

1. What type of job evaluation will be carried out?
   - ■ ascertaining job surveys, which describe the current situation;
   - ■ normative job surveys, in which jobs on the basis of their mutual relationships are linked into a logically coherent body;

- structuring surveys which focus on the issue: What is the ideal situation for this organisation in terms of objectives, results and responsibilities on the one hand and job-related development opportunities for employees on the other hand?

2. How valid are the job characteristics? Do they differentiate sufficiently in the interpretation of definitions to prevent the same requirement from being evaluated or weighted twice?

3. Are the results reproducible, ie can the justifications of the results clearly and repeatedly be derived from the definitions of the method so that a correct comparison can be made where a re-evaluation is necessary?

4. Has the method sufficient and clearly recognisable benchmark jobs suitable for the organisation?

5. What options has the organisation if an employee does not meet the requirements as laid down in the job description?

6. Does the organisation intend to create or develop skills of its own in evaluating jobs, or does it prefer to use external experts? What are the arguments for its choice?

7. Which objectives are being pursued with the implementation of job evaluation?

8. Have the procedures been carefully constructed?

9. In which way are aspects of the job evaluation process communicated to employees, labour representatives and management?

10. Does the organisation have previous experience in job evaluation? With which obstacles and disadvantages has the organisation then been confronted?

3

Job evaluation systems

3.1 INTRODUCTION

The previous chapter ended with a checklist which may assist in making the correct choices/considerations when an organisation plans to implement job evaluation or to switch to another method. However having satisfied all the questions in this checklist does not mean that the selection process has been concluded or that a final choice can be made. This requires insight in the job evaluation methods currently offered in the market. Acquiring the necessary information is not an easy task, mainly because system-holders do not provide access to the details of the method before a serious assignment seems to be within reach. If an organisation does succeed in obtaining comprehensive information, comparisons are hampered by the fact that the characteristics of one method are more or less detailed than those of other methods. As a consequence the definitions of various methods are hardly comparable.

In Europe more than 100 different methods of job evaluation are presently being used. A number of these have been developed specifically for a particular company or organisation, others are being offered in the market by specialised firms. Others again are a mixture of both. The methods can be divided roughly into two main groups:

— methods based upon an evaluation of jobs based on a points system;
— methods that determine the weight of jobs by comparing them with a general description of levels of similar jobs (reasoned comparison). A more subtle approach is provided in Tables 3.1 and 3.2.

In order to make a detailed judgement of various methods an *analytical survey on the basis of their features* has been made which also includes a description of the evaluation characteristics used in each

Table 3.1 *Various methods for job evaluation classified according to characteristics*

		2. Method of determining grades		
		2a Ranking of jobs	2b Classifying of jobs into classes	2c Scale or matrix
1. Characteristics or entire job to be assessed	1a Various characteristics	Ranking per characteristic (factor comparison)		Assigning per character (point factor)
	1b One characteristic only		Decision band method	Time span method
	1c Job as a whole	Job ranking	Job classification	

method. Next, details are given of the various *characteristics* of each. Finally, information is provided on the *perspective* from which these evaluation characteristics are built. The survey does not pretend to be exhaustive, only to provide an overview of the major aspects of various evaluation methods. Where appropriate, a block describing inconveniences (or working conditions) can be added to the analyses.

Under the heading 'specific system information' some additional information is given, including:

- system technique;
- procedures/implementation;
- tools/computer support.

At the end of each method some representative parts of the grading or evaluation tables are included. On the one hand these give some idea as to how the table is constructed and on the other hand they show typical elements of the evaluation method. In order to be sure that the information on the various methods is well understood and correctly interpreted, we have presented these descriptions of the methods to their owners for their comments. In particular concerning

Table 3.2   *Classification of the job evaluation methods discussed according to characteristics and the benefits and disadvantages*

Type	Characteristic	Benefits	Disadvantages
Non analytical			
Ranking	Comparing entire jobs in order to arrive at a ranking	Easy to use and easy to understand	No well-defined standard and therefore difficult to explain and to defend
Paired comparison	Each job is compared with all other jobs, scores are assigned (eg 0 = lighter, 1 = equal, 2 = heavier) then added together to find a total score for the jobs	Reasonably reliable	See ranking
Grading/ classifying job level	On the basis of a standard description and/or grading (ie an interpretation of certain factors such as independence, know-how, etc) an entire job is compared with a standard job description or grading	Simple to use provided the gradings for each level are practicable and well described and that sample jobs are appropriate to the organisation	Difficult to put into effect for complex jobs, because the description does not apply and/or the inter-pretation of factors used in grading become too complex and too abstract.
Analytical/ points	Several factors are chosen that are considered important for establishing the weight of the job; for each factor a score is determined after which scores of indi-vidual factors will be translated into a total score of the job.	Defining factors clearly avoids subjec-tivity and facilitates establishing (and defending) differ-ences between jobs. This is particularly so if differences are established through techniques from observational psychology	Rather difficult to implement and main-tain; objectivity is illusive; a subjective assessment is needed for scoring each factor.

the information under the heading 'specific system information', the author has for a major part depended upon data provided by the system holders.

The growing possibilities and use of the computer and the occasional automated job evaluation system already in existence were discussed in the previous chapter. For the sake of completeness more detailed information on the individual method has been included under the heading 'specific system information'.

A second remarkable aspect is that system-holders increasingly respond to the demands in the market. Methods of several 'levels' are being offered, varying from very elaborate to simplified versions that require rather less specialist knowledge in this field. However, such simplifications may also enforce an intimate link between the 'applier' (management) and the (internal or external) 'specialist' in order to ensure consistency and comparability with the external market.

For a proper understanding of the descriptions of the methods and the details appended, it should be kept in mind that the job evaluation process consists of several steps:

1. *Job analysis.* The process of inquiring into the content of the job and recording the relevant information for evaluating/grading the job.
2. *Job evaluation method.* Evaluating/grading or weighing of job by means of evaluating, weighing or measuring instrument.
3. *Testing the ranking.* This ranking is the result of listing jobs according to the value of their final score.
4. *Establishing grades.* This is done on the basis of the ranking list and the scatter diagram in such a way that within each job family clusters of jobs are obtained which are similar in terms of their weight and level.

Before starting to analyse/compare a number of job evaluation methods we give some explanation of the aspects of these analysis/comparisons. As noted before, this chapter presents a survey of methods on the basis of respectively their 'features' and 'characteristics', 'factors' and 'aspects', a model which in general can be applied to all job evaluation methods. The four 'main characteristics' are :

- Know-how
- Problem solving
- Area of responsibility
- Working conditions

However, there are some methods that are quite difficult to fit into this model. System-holders have rightly pointed out that what for their methods is listed under 'features' for purposes of comparison is, in fact, a typical 'characteristic'. Other methods have grouped a number of 'characteristics' or 'factors' under one collective term, without giving a precise definition of that term. The profile of each method as to its main characteristics, factors and aspects therefore needs some explanation.

The starting point of the analyses model is the following model. A *characteristic* of the method comprises one or more *factors* which in their turn can be separated into *aspects*. An example:

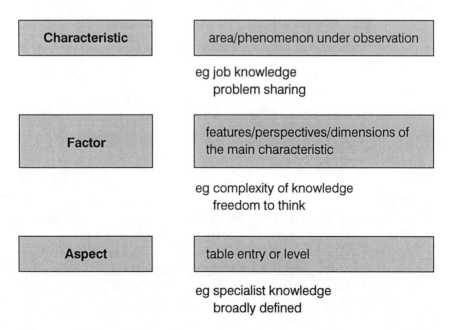

Most methods operate with matrix tables for each 'characteristic' in which the horizontal and vertical axis have been named and defined. These axis are called 'factors', which have different levels (or degrees) and are what we call 'aspects'. These levels, which constitute the table entries (see Figure 3.1) are also defined separately.

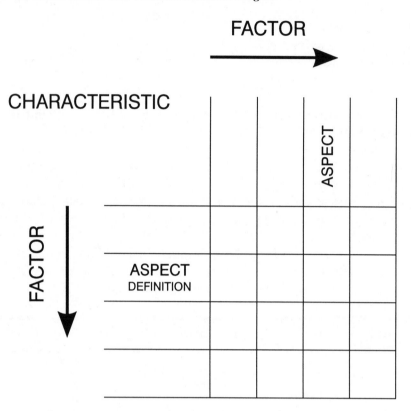

Figure 3.1: *Basic layout of a matrix table*

As previously stated, this model cannot be used for all job evaluation methods; occasionally the main characteristics have not been defined. In order to obtain some insight into these methods the indication/name preferred by the system-holder is given between brackets, after the headings 'characteristic', 'factor' and 'aspect'

The comparative profile gives a summary of the 'features' of the job the method analyses, name of the 'characteristics' as used by the system-holder, and the 'factors/aspects' for each characteristic. This profile has been standardised to some extent in order to facilitate comparisons. All job evaluation methods discussed in this chapter have been rearranged to fit in the set-up in Table 3.3. These methods are:

Hay   Hay Management Consultants
EFP   Watson Wyatt
Framework   Towers Perrin

Table 3.3   *Analytical model for comparing job evaluation systems*

Features	Characteristics	Factors/aspects
Know-how	• Know-how/skills	• Theoretical know-how/ experiences in the job • Skills, experience in using equipment, etc.
	• Managerial aspects	• Ability to organise people and means
	• Human relation skills	• Different contacts • Written communication skills
Problem solving	• Thinking framework	• Freedom to think in finding solutions for problems
	• Complexity • Creativity	• Analytical judgement • Thinking challenge
Areas of responsibility	• Level of decision making • Magnitude	• Freedom to act • Project realisation
Inconveniences	• Use of physical power • Exertion • Personnel risks	

Note: If the characteristic is listed under more than one headings, this indicates that the characteristic contains dimensions which fit several descriptions

The profile consists of the following elements:

The *features*. In order to perform the job the job-holder is required to possess some knowledge/properties/skills necessary to solve the problems which occur within the job in order to achieve the intended objectives which represent the responsibility of the job.

The *characteristics*. These are the elements which define the main knowledge/properties/skills, but they also indicate what the method has defined as main problems of the job and what constitutes the area of responsibility. They also demonstrate how the method classifies the various factors/aspects and assesses the interrelationships.

The *factors/aspects* give an impression of the degree of refinement and detail of the method. More important they show what and how the methods wants to 'measure' in a job.

3.2 HAY GUIDE CHARTS, HAY MANAGEMENT CONSULTANTS

Table 3.4: *Characteristics, factors/aspects of the Hay Guide Chart and Profile Method*

Features	Characteristics	Factors/aspects
Know-how	● Know-how	● Technical know-how, eg: – advanced vocational – basic professional – seasoned professional ● Breadth of management know-how, eg: – activity – heterogeneous ● Human relations skills eg: – important
Problem solving	● Problem solving	● Thinking environment – freedom to think, eg: – standardised – clearly defined ● Thinking challenge, eg: – patterned – adaptive
Areas of responsibility	● Accountability	● Freedom to act, eg: – regulated – directed ● Area and type of impact, eg: – magnitude
Inconveniences	– Physical effort and/or strain – Working environment – Hazards	

In the model of the comparative profile of methods on page 77 under the heading 'Characteristics' the text 'know-how/skills' has been put in a darkened box to indicate that this characteristic will be elaborated according to 'Factors' (middle grey) and table entries or 'Aspects' (light grey).

Finally, we would like to point out that the profiles could only be made in such detail thanks to the wholehearted co-operation of system-holders by providing all system information.

Specific system information

System technique

- No weights. The relative 'weighing factors' are implied in the relative value of aspects.
- For each level of 'steps' on the evaluation charts a definition and a short explanation of the concept concerned is given.
- Through the job profiles the method has a built-in check on the results of the evaluation. In addition, the profiles provide useful information on organisational interrelationships, the characteristic of the job, etc.

Procedures/implementation

- The Hay method considers the determination of the job levels as being a responsibility of the management. The evaluating of jobs (in the sense of attributing 'value' to jobs) is carried out by an evaluation committee in which management, the personnel – function on the basis of its functional responsibility – and representatives of Hay participate to support and guide the process and monitor the correct implementation of the method.
- In the implementation process the Hay Group is responsible for the application of the correct standards of the Hay method in view of the external comparability. The support by the system-holder during the maintenance phase also depends upon the skills and competence of the company itself. The Hay Group recommends performing an annual check on the standards being used. In any case, the Hay Group itself will carry out such a check when the company participates (each year) in the Hay Dynamic Pay Survey.

Tools/computer support

- The Hay Group has developed several forms of computer aided job evaluation under the collective name of HRXpert. Depending upon the demands of the company these systems can be employed with respect to:

- speed/costs of the implementation/maintenance;
- dynamics of change of the organisation/jobs
- methods of format in which job characteristics must be achieved;
- a standalone justification of remuneration. Alternatively, it may be used as an integral part of the HRM system;
- the degree of centralisation or decentralisation of job evaluation.

Characteristics	Factors	Aspects

Know-how

Definition

Know-how is the sum of every kind of knowledge, skill and experience required for standard acceptable job performance. It is the fund of knowledge (however required) which is necessary for meeting:

- The requirement for know-how in practical procedures, specialised techniques and professional disciplines
- The requirement for know-how in integrating and harmonising the diverse elements involved in managerial situations. This know-how may be exercised in an advisory capacity as well as excessively. It involves combining to some degree the elements of planning, organising, directing, controlling and innovating and takes account of size, functional or organisational diversity, and time scale.
- The requirement for know-how in working with and through people (within or outside the organisation)

Guide Chart for Know-How

	Planning, Organising, Controlling Breadth of management know-how								
Technical	0 Task			I Activity			III Heterogeneous		
Know-how	1	2	3	1	2	3	1	2	3
A Primary	38	43	50	50	57	66	87	100	115
	43	50	57	57	66	76	100	115	132
	50	57	66	66	76	87	115	132	152
E Basic Professional				152	175	200			
				175	200	230			
				200	230	264			

Human relations skills

1. Basic	2. Important	3. Critical

Samples of definitions of: *technical know-how:*

A. Primary

> Jobs requiring secondary education only; plus some working indoctrination

Explanation of definition for A:

Jobs falling into this slot are extremely simple in nature, and can be learned within a matter of several days/weeks. Little formal education is required.

E. Basic professional

> Jobs requiring sufficiency in technical, scientific or specialised field based on understanding of concepts and principles normally associated with a professional or academic qualification or gained through a detailed grasp of involved practices and procedures

Explanation of definition for E:

This slot is generally represented by basic college education or advanced vocational skills strengthened by years of on the job experience. It relies on the job need to have a specialised body of knowledge at the incumbent's command, like engineering, personnel, production management, underwriting, credit extension, etc.

Samples of definitions of *breadth of managerial know-how*

I Activity

> Performance or supervision of work which is specific as to objective and content with appropriate awareness of related activities

Explanation of definition for I:

Covered by this category are all non-managerial positions, ie both individual performers and supervisors.

III   Heterogeneous

> Operational or conceptual integration of functions which are diverse in nature and in objective in an important management area, or central co-ordination of a strategic function

Explanation of definition for III:

This category covers multi-functional managers. By multi-functional we mean either:
1. managing at least two functional areas of an important nature and size, or
2. diversity in the nature of the end results of each area is important, and
3. focusing on competing requirements.

Samples of definitions of *human relations skills*

2   Important

> Understanding, influencing and communication with people are important but not overriding considerations

Explanation of definition for 2:

The HR skills are not overriding to the success of an assignment. However, normal courtesy and effectiveness with people is just not enough to carry the job. 2 HR skills involve interplay with subordinates and superiors of a more critical nature. This slot is awarded to positions that have to do some co-ordinating outside the incumbent's unit or company organisation.

Problem solving

Definition

> Problem solving is the 'self starting' thinking required by the job for analysing, evaluating, creating, reasoning, arriving at and drawing conclusions. To the extent that thinking is circumscribed by standards or covered by precedents, or referred to others, problem solving is diminished.
>
> Problem solving has two dimensions:
> - The environment in which the thinking takes place
> - The challenge presented by thinking to be done

Guide chart for problem solving

	Thinking challenge		
Freedom to think	2 Patterned	3 Variable	5 Uncharted
A Strict routine	14% 16%	19% 22%	
F. Broadly defined		38% 43%	66% 76%

Samples of definitions of *freedom to think*

A. Strict routine

> Thinking within detailed rules, instructions and/or rigid supervision

Explanation of definition for A:

Rules are very basic and instructions quite specific (mostly oral orders). Example: 'File only red copies'; dispatch mail on hand at 3 and 6 pm; mail according to class and weight rate schedule; sweep hallway and return for further work.

F. Broadly defined

> Thinking within broad policies and objectives, under general direction

Explanation of definition for F:

The determination of the 'what to do' in applying broad policies to solve the problem is largely left up to the incumbent. However, the objectives themselves would tend to be stated specifically, ie attains a 10 per cent ROI.

Samples of definitions of *thinking challenge*

2. Patterned

> Similar situations requiring solution by discriminating choice of things learned

Explanation of definition for 2:

Here we are confronted with a mix and match situation. The majority of non-exempt jobs are covered by this slot. Example: sorting 20 grey balls into three shades of grey.

3. Variable

> Differing situations requiring the identification and selection of solutions through the application of acquired knowledge

Explanation of definition for 3:

Interpolative implies being confronted with a number of different questions, each having several different answers to it. It is in other words, a pick and choose situation. Decisions can still be made rather rapidly based on prior knowledge or experience as opposed to fitting a prescribed pattern, or the necessity to define the problem and solution more methodically.

Computer support

HRXpert is the software used with the Hay Guide Chart and Profile Method. It can be required as a full system or in modules, with the following utilities:

■ Work comparison/job evaluation (example displays already shown);

- performance management;
- competency analyses;
- comparison design and administration.

HRXpert is a decision-making support tool which enables organisations to address today's HR issues: work comparison, compensation administration, performance management, and human resources planning and development. As far as job evaluation is concerned the following modules of HRXpert are of interest:

Chart

Chart provides you with on-line record keeping and reporting for Hay Guide Chart evaluation and documentation. This module provides you with:

- a display-based Hay Guide Chart tailored for your organisation;
- a data viewing tool providing you with the most relevant comparisons to other jobs or positions;
- a documentation area to record position description data, evaluation rationales, and other information;
- an ability to evaluate jobs, positions, or individuals using multiple work comparison models.

Some examples of displays are shown in Tables 3.5, 3.6 and 3.7:

Comparison

Comparison is a factor-based approach to evaluating work. The software can complement any evaluation methodology which uses a set of common factors for job or position evaluation. This approach facilitates the slotting of jobs, positions, or employees quickly against a series of benchmarks based on direct comparisons for each factor employed in the work comparison process. The use of an accepted and comprehensive benchmark sample minimises subjectivity in assessment. It helps to ensure consistency in evaluation as much as possible through an easy and intuitive measurement process. Comparison helps in:

- quick evaluation with relevant job information readily available;
- evaluation by line management with HR assistance, without a full understanding of the Hay method.
- decentralised evaluation of nonbenchmark positions.

Table 3.5: *Evaluating know-how*

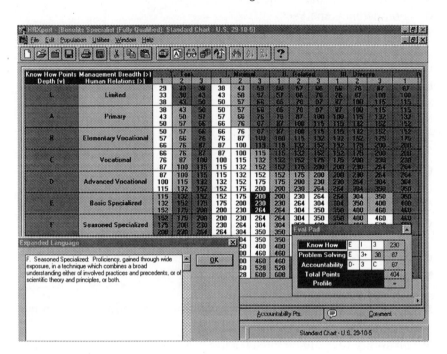

Questionnaires

Hay designs tailor-made questionnaires to generate relevant job
or role information for various purposes, like defining pay levels,
supporting people development and person/job matching. This chapter provides you with three examples of job size establishing questionnaires and one example of a mixed model. For establishing job
size Hay offers three approaches: 'comparison', 'job family' and
'universal'.

Table 3.6: *Comparing the job evaluation under consideration with other (or selection of) job evaluations.*

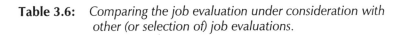

An example of a problem-solving scale:

Problem solving consists of the mental processes involved in thinking about work to be done as well as the organisational constraints in which the thinking takes place	
4. Instructions usually provide latitude to consider variations in the sequence of procedures based on the situation at hand	Telephone operator A Receptionist/switchboard operator File clerk A
5.	
6. These jobs are confronted with multiple choice situations and through prior exposure/experience have learned which choice is the most appropriate solution	Payroll clerk A General clerk A Accounting clerk B
7.	

Table 3.7: *Comparison model to judge the validity of the score for know-how*

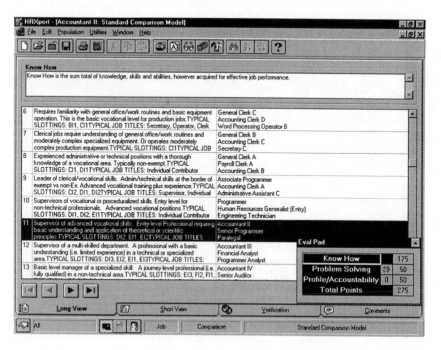

How is a Comparison questionnaire organised?

When a benchmark of jobs is evaluated with the Hay method of job evaluation and profiling, subsequent jobs can then easily be slotted in by focusing solely on know-how, problem solving and short profile. The questionnaire can be used to ask line management to indicate the requirement levels of know-how and problem solving and indicate the correct short profile. Line management is supported in this task by showing which jobs are already slotted in at a certain level, hence the name 'comparison'. An evaluation committee reviews outcomes to ensure internal equity.

How is a Job-family questionnaire organised?

A job-family questionnaire focuses solely on a set of jobs that have a common job purpose which can be fulfilled at several levels, eg technicians.

A job family questionnaire may have a strong developmental focus: aspiring technicians can see what the next step up the ladder looks like. An example of questionnaire content is:

Job-family questions:
   1. Technical knowledge and expertise
   2. Technical diversity/breadth
   3. Integration of technical disciplines
   4. Knowledge transfer
   5. Complexity of projects
   6. People management
   7. Communication

Generic questions:
   8. Problem analysis
   9. Level of thinking
   10. Time frame

Impossible or unlikely combinations of answers can be flagged by computer warnings.

An example of the knowledge transfer scale:

Select the item that best describes the degree to which the job is expected to contribute to results through the transfer of knowledge
5. The job is responsible for communicating knowledge which impacts on business operations and transfer of knowledge by teaching team members on the job
6.
7. The job is a consulting resource in transferring technology to outside the unit
8.
9. The job is responsible for organising and securing know-how transfer on a large scale by developing the appropriate processes and programmes for communication to ensure sustained/improved business results

How is a Universal questionnaire organised?

A universal questionnaire is also a tailor-made questionnaire, its universal character being that it targets the entire job set of a company. Its broad focus necessitates a larger number of questions. The list below shows a possible table of content and what Hay job evaluation factor the questions relate to:

Questionnaire item	Hay job evaluation factor
1. Primary focus of my position	Profile
2. Position objectives	Freedom to act
3. Overall knowledge	Know-how depth
4. Education and experience (minimum)	Know-how depth
5. Communication and interpersonal skills	Human relations skills
6. Customer service skills	Human relations skills
7. Management and planning skills	Know-how breadth
8. Organisation and integration of tasks	Know-how breadth
9. Management responsibilities	Human relations skills Magnitude/impact
10. Functional/technical responsibilities	Know-how depth
11. Training and development responsibilities	Human relations skills
12. Judgement and problem-solving skills	Problem-solving environment
13. Problem complexity	Problem-solving challenge
14. Decision-making responsibilities	Freedom to act
15. Direct influence	Magnitude/impact
16. Indirect influence	Magnitude/impact

Here again, impossible or unlikely combinations of answers can be flagged by computer warnings.

An example of a management responsibilities scale:

Please read each statement below carefully and then select the one that best describes the way that the position contributes to the management and performance improvement of others. Please note that these statements are not ranked in any order or hierarchy
1. I am accountable for the supervision of a group or team of permanent reports. I assign work, monitor progress and ensure the quality and timeliness of output
2. My role is project team leader or project manager. I have no permanent direct reports but I am responsible for ensuring that project members understand the work assigned and have sufficient resources available to meet their objectives. Project members may include external consultants and/or contractors
3. Although there are no employees reporting directly to me, I am responsible for helping, guiding and advising others. I may also provide on-the-job training

How is a Mixed model questionnaire organised?

A mixed model questionnaire integrates information necessary for establishing job size as well as establising required levels of competences in order to match persons to jobs and to support personal development. Added to the job family questions or universal questions are questions that capture competency levels. These may include:

11. Influencing others
12. Sensitivity to people
13. Concern for quality
14. Getting results
15. Being flexible
16. Etc.

3.3 EVALUATION FRAMEWORK, TOWERS PERRIN

Table 3.8: *Characteristics, factors/aspects of framework*

Features	Characteristics (basic)	Factors/aspects
Know-how	■ Knowledge and skills ■ Human relations	■ Tailor-made, designed for client
Problem solving	■ Problem solving	
Areas of responsibilities	■ Freedom to act ■ Accountabilities	See examples from the banking and retail industry

Specific system information

System technique

- Framework is a 'point factor' job evaluation scheme customised to client requirements.
- Framework uses a tailored questionnaire to collect information on the above factors.
- Framework uses a computer system that stores questionnaire responses and allows easy manipulation of the data for:
  - data checking;
  - calculating factor levels and points;
  - reporting results.

- In the context of Framework the 'characteristics' (see Table 3.8 above) comprises a group of wider elements in the sense that there are no 'fixed' or well-defined characteristics that can be split into the same factors/aspects. Examples of a tailor-made application are shown in Tables 3.9 and 3.10:

Table 3.9: *Example of Framework set-up for a financial organisation*

Know-how	■ knowledge and skills	A ■ education, experience, skills, knowledge and expertise
	■ resource responsibility	F ■ direct reports (number and nature of responsibility) ■ projected/ad-hoc teams
	■ contacts	C ■ external level and nature ■ internal level and nature
Problem solving	■ problem solving	B ■ complexity of problems
Areas of responsibility	■ freedom of action	D ■ freedom of action
	■ accountabilities	E ■ accountability for managing projects and processes
	■ resource responsibility	F ■ financial
	■ impact	G ■ internal ■ external and business impact

Table 3.10: *Example of Framework set-up for a retail organisation*

Know-how	■ professional/technical ■ skills and knowledge	1A education and experience 1B: level of expertise 1C: specific job skills

	■ management
	   responsibilities
		5A: number of employees
		5B: level of responsibility
		         for staff

	■ communications	4A: external communications
Problem solving	■ work complexity	2A: problem solving 2B: independence and initiative
Areas of responsibility	■ decision making	3A: job's own decisions 3B: advising other's decisions

	■ management
	   responsibilities
		5C: level of financial
		         responsibility
		5D: nature of financial
		         responsibility

	■ business impact	6A: potential positive
		         impact
		6B: potential negative
		         impact

Procedures/implementation

■ Procedures are established after consultation and in collaboration with the organisation. Securing a maximum involvement of the employees concerned and if possible of worker representatives is considered advisable as it increases the acceptance and support.

■ Each characteristic in the job evaluation scheme can be broken down into its factors/aspects and each of these factors/aspects is broken down into questions for the questionnaire. For each job being evaluated, the system uses the responses to each of these specific questions and determines the factor level required.

■ Information on jobs can be collected through questionnaires or structured interviews, depending on the situation and agreed process for the job evaluation exercise.

- The basis of the scoring process is provided by one or a combination of the following items which have been chosen in consultation with the client:
  - multiple regression against a reference rank order of benchmark jobs which is agreed with the client;
  - using Towers Perrin's knowledge of typical distributions of weighting within schemes;
  - agreeing an initial set of weights with the client based on the perceived importance of the various factors;
  - starting from a basis of equal weighting for each factor and then trying alternative models to better reflect the relative importance of the various factors.
- Modelling is made easy through the Framework software.

Tools/computer support

Processing the completed questionnaires is fully automated.

- Framework software is a complete package for job evaluation, competencies and remuneration.
- An extensive report generator is available, providing a range of standard reports and the facility to create tailor-made reports. With this generator summaries can be made that provide insight into the interrelationships and consistency of the evaluation of jobs.

Samples of questionnaires, from different organisations, designed after consultation with the client (including samples of Response Tables):

Knowledge and skills

A. *Level of formal/academic training*
Consider the levels of education and qualifications required for this job:

1. What is the minimum essential level of qualification?
2. What is the *desirable* or optimum level of qualification?

	Response Table A
A	PhD or equivalent
B	
C	
D	
E	Three to five GCSEs or equivalent/NVO level 2
F	One to two GCSEs or equivalent/NVO level 1
G	
H	

B. Job-related experience and training

Now consider the period of prior, relevant work experience and necessary on-the-job training:

3. What is the minimum necessary total period of prior experience and training?
4. What is the desirable or optimum total period of prior experience and training?

	Response Table B
A	More than 5 years
B	
C	7–12 months
D	
E	Less than 1 month

Knowledge and skills

C. Level of proficiency
This section focuses on the level of proficiency required to successfully hold the position being evaluated.

Determine a position's level of proficiency by matching the job family's career progression to *Response Table B*. The entry-level position in the job family (eg Junior Accountant) would normally be a level 'E', Junior Practitioner, but may be at a level 'F', Apprentice/Trainee.

Supervisory and subordinate positions may have the same level of proficiency; do not automatically give a higher response to the supervisor.

This question is intended to capture technical expertise, not managerial authority. This is considered elsewhere in the questionnaire.

While general management is sometimes considered a job family, this will not be appropriate for determining the level of proficiency since these positions are normally attained only after considerable experience in a functional area such as marketing, production or finance. The level of proficiency for a General Manager should be determined within the context of a normal career progression leading to the general management position.

This question is concerned with technical expertise, and not managerial authority. The recognised expert will be that person who is regarded as having the greatest technical knowledge in a particular area – not necessarily the manager of that area.

5. Within the position family, this position *requires* the following demonstrated level of proficiency.

Response Table C

A Leading expert – acts as final source of expertise over a major portion of the organisation, or external to the organisation

B

C

D Practitioner – works independently on assignments of standard difficulty for the vocation, profession, trade or craft

E

F Apprentice/Trainee – work assignments provide training and development

---

D. *Physical/operational skills*

6. Select a statement from A to E in Response Table D which best describes the physical/operational skills needed for your job.

Response Table D

A Physical skills may be used, but little training is required

B

C

D

E High levels of dexterity and physical skills are needed to interpret programme operational requirements in environments that require speed, accuracy, adaptation and reaction to rapidly changing circumstances

---

Problem solving

E. *Fact-finding and analyses*

Fact-finding and analyses may compromise a very small or very large part of a job. The statements in this section seek to establish the degree of fact-finding and analyses required as well as its nature.

This section requires the use of response 'A' *once only*. To facilitate completion of this section, find the statements that match response 'A' first. Then use the other responses as appropriate; responses 'B', 'C' and 'D' may be used more than once.

For each of the statements below (7 to 11), select from Response Table E the level appropriate for this job.

7. Problems are comparatively familiar and well-defined, and primarily focused on a specific work function. Typically a number of possible solutions are apparent, based mainly on precedents and/or established processes
8.
9.
10. Problems are complex and may affect many business units. Problem-solving complexity may result from: *either*: the variable and diverse nature of problems encountered in rapidly changing situations *or*: the fundamental, in-depth and long-term nature of a range of specialist problems.
11. Problems are highly complex and cover a very wide range of issues across the company. Problem solving typically requires a thorough understanding of complex and interrelated business issues across the organisation.

	Response Table E
A	Most applicable
B	Applicable on many occasions
C	Applicable on a few occasions
D	Rarely or never applicable

F. *Innovation and initiative*

This section seeks information about the job's responsibility for *innovative* thinking. Many jobs do not demand any innovative thinking, but some do. For example, any job that requires an individual to design new products or methods, write informational technical publications, perform research in previously unexamined areas or find new ways of making money requires innovative thinking. *These examples have a common feature: the absence of guides or procedures to follow.*

One of the four statements must be rated 'A', with 'B', 'C' and 'D' used as often as appropriate.

One of the following four statements must be rated 'A'. Read all four statements, select the one most important to the position and mark that statement as 'A'. Responses 'B', 'C' or 'D' may be used more than once.

12. Some creative thinking needed to vary or adapt standard procedures to meet different circumstances.

13.

14.

15. Creative thinking is a fundamental requirement for realisation of broadly specified briefs. May also be required to investigate and instigate new ways of enhancing and improving existing techniques.

16. Innovation and original thinking required to originate or develop new theories, principles, concepts and policies and their application.

Response Table F
A   Most applicable
B   Applicable on many occasions
C   Applicable on a few occasions
D   Rarely or never applicable

Another example of a questionnaire:

Factor 1 – Professional/technical skills and knowledge

Factor 2 – Work complexity

2B: Independence and initiative

This section considers the requirements to act independently and to display personal initiative in the job. It considers both the degree and nature of independence. Is the job largely driven by procedures and precedents, in which case an 'A' response at Q18 or 19 would be required? Or is it one in which creativity and individual initiative constantly has to be applied, a job with the purpose of coming up with new ideas and approaches, which would lead to an 'A' response at Q22 or, exceptionally Q23?

Remember that the 'A' response must be used only once, and the 'B' response no more than twice. Examples of a benchmark job scoring an A at Q23 would be Store Manager I, and the A at Q22 would be Store Manager II.

Consider the requirement for independent action and the use of initiative in effectively addressing the activities, issues and problems which arise in the job.

Allocate response 'A' to the level of independence and initiative described below in questions 18 to 23 which is most applicable to the job. *Use this response only once.*

Then allocate response 'B' to the level(s) which are important but not predominant features of the independence and initiative required by the job-holder. *Use this response no more than twice.*

Finally, allocate responses 'C' and 'D' to the other levels as appropriate.

Q18	Work requires accurate adherence to established practices and procedures and is subject to close external guidance. There is no or little requirement for individual initiative or judgement
Q19	
Q20	Work follows precedent and procedures in the main and external guidance is available. Some use of initiative is required, for example in tailoring work practices and in responding to unexpected circumstances
Q21	Guidelines exist but there is a fair degree of operational independence. Regular use of initiative is required, for example in the development of improved work methods, and enhancing existing operations, affecting the job-holder and possibly colleagues
Q22	
Q23	The job, to a large extent, is independent and self-driven within broad policy guidelines, and only results are reviewed. High levels of initiative and creativity are essential, for example in implementing new business policies and approaches, and developing new ideas to achieve broad business goals

Response Table
Independence and initiative
A   The predominant requirement for independence and initiative which is most applicable to the job (use this response only once)
B   A secondary significant but not predominant aspect of the initiative and independence required in the job (use this response no more than twice)
C   An occasional level of independence and initiative required
D   Not required or a rare insignificant level of independence and initiative in the job

Example of a financial organisation:

(In this example problem solving is designed in a way that meets the needs in a financial organisation.)

B: Problem solving

1. Consider the complexity of problems which the job has to deal with.
2. For each of the questions below, select a response from the Response table which is most appropriate to the job.
3. Use responses A and B once only (do not use B at all if it does not apply to this job)
4. Use responses A and B once only (do not use B at all if it does not apply to this job). You may use responses C and D as often as required
5. Please complete all the boxes.

Original thinking and creativity

Q10	The job requires clear instructions to be followed with limited scope for individual initiative, original thought or action
Q11	
Q12	Creative thinking is required to develop new or improved solutions to a limited range of problems or to parts of existing processes and procedures
Q13	Creative thinking is required to develop new or improved solutions or working methods across a range of diverse circumstances or to change existing processes and procedures
Q14	
Q15	High levels of innovation and original thinking required. Work involves developing new concepts and theories in areas with potentially wide application in the organisation and/or externally, for example in new policy development, or addressing unique, complex and intractable operational issues

---

Response Table: Problem solving

A   Most applicable to this job
B   Applicable on many occasions
C   Applicable on a few occasions
D   Rarely or never applicable

Factor 3 – Decision making

Factor 4 – Communications

Example of a retail organisation

This factor is concerned with the nature of the communications and contacts which the job-holder has with people inside and outside the organisation in order to carry out their job effectively. It includes all business-related communication or interaction, whether connected face-to-face, by telephone or in writing, which is relevant to the job. It considers the nature of contacts and the communication skills required in relation to external audiences and groups on this page, and internal staff overleaf. When responding to all questions, remember to:

- exclude from consideration any purely incidental, non-business related contacts, for example in lunch breaks;
- also exclude general contacts which are desirable but not essential to effective job performance, such as certain staff being encouraged to walk around and 'be seen' by customers;
- exclude also contacts with the job's immediate superior and subordinates, which are considered under other factors.

In the statements a relationship is defined as being a contact over an extended period of time.

4A: External communications

4B: Internal communications

Factor 5 – Managerial responsibilities

5A: Number of employees

5B   Level of responsibilities for staff

5C   Level of financial responsibilities

5D Nature of financial responsibilities

Factor 6 – Business impact

6A Potential positive impact

6B Potential negative impact

The result of the evaluation, after completion of the questionnaire by different judges, like the superior, the evaluation committee, the incumbent, is given in Table 3.11 below.

Table 3.11: *Sample of an evaluation using Framework*

Job: PA44			Publicity Officer				Structure: Operations Grade: Op 8		
Profile number	S	I	C	M	D	Profile number	1*	2	3
1. Communicating ideas	C	E	E	E	2	Accountabilities	170	259	268
2. Services and advice	C	D	E		2	Human relations	56	89	75
3. Financial resources	A	B	C		2	Problem solving	135	166	170
4. Physical resources	B	D	B	B	2	Freedom to act	27	38	38
5. Supervision of staff	B	A	A	A	1	Impact	27	44	38
						Knowledge and skills	91	217	172
10. Problem solving	B	B	D	B	2				
						Total points	560	813	761
						Profiler:			
12. Amount of freedom	C	C	D	C	1	1 = Supervisor			
						2 = Committee			
13. Internal impact	D	D	C	D	1	3 = Incumbent			
14. External impact	E	E	D	E	1				

Key:
S = Supervisor   M = Mode
C = Committee   I = Incumbent
D = Deviation
* = Authorised profile

The so-called 'up-down comparator' is another check that can be made on how to respond to one job to others in the same job family.

Each column of responses on the report represents the responses from separate jobs. The first column is the job which the position under review is being supervised by; the second is the job under review; the remaining columns relate to subordinates of the job-holder.

The first column shows the question name. Where the questions are underlined, it means that there is an unusual relationship between the responses for the job under review and those of the manager and/or subordinates. Typically, it means that the job-holder has responses at a lower level than his/her subordinates, or higher than his/her manager.

The final section compares the 'factor' points across the jobs being compared. This enables the user to identify the factors that are valued differently between the jobs. So, the up-down comparator is a useful tool for designing new jobs to fit within the existing job hierarchy or to examine anomalies in job design.

Table 3.12 *Second sample evaluation*

Selected Job:	Senior Publicity Officer reports to Chief Publicity Officer						
Job:					Profile		
PA28	Chief publicity officer				*1 Analyst		
PB36	Senior publicity officer				*1 Supervisor		
PA44	Publicity officer				*1 Supervisor		

Questions	PA 28 1	PB 36 1	PA 44 1	Factor points	PA 28	PB 36	PA 44
1. Communicating ideas	E	D	C	Accountabilities	283	220	170
2. Services and advice	D	D	C	Human relations	77	60	56
3. Financial resources	C	A	A	Problem solving	146	141	135
4. Physical resources	C	B	B	Freedom to act	38	38	27
5A Supervision of staff	D	C	B	Impact	50	33	27
5B Number of staff	D	B	B	Knowledge and skills	154	145	91
6A Supervision –ad hoc teams	A	A	B				
6B Number involved	A	A	B	Total	748	637	506
7A Contacts – own department	C	C	B				
7B Contacts – other areas	F	C	C				
7C Contacts – trade unions	A	A	A				
8A Contacts – public	B	B	C				
10B Problem solving	C	C	B				
10C PS – Influenced by precedent	A	A	A				
11B CT – Limited problems	B	B	C				
11E Innovative	D	D	D				
14 External Impact	E	D	E				

Key:
* = Authorised profile

The following pages will show a number of displays to give more insight of the design of the Framework software

Table 3.13: *Framework: Available reports.*
This display shows the various reports that are available (as illustrated in the 'sampler'). Organisations can develop their own reports using the 'Quest' report writer tool.

Table 3.14: *Framework: Factor points and job profile.*
This just shows the two main areas in which data is held ('Jobs and Profiles').
Job profiles can be challenged to look for inconsistent responses.
Only one profile can be the 'Master' profile for the job, even if multiple
profiles are recorded.

Towers Perrin FRAMEWORK

File   Edit   Query   Window   Help

ANALYST PROGRAMM   Database   Demo 2.2

Factor Points

Factor	Points
ACCOUNTABILITIES	179
HUMAN RELATIONS	46
PROBLEM SOLVING	125
FREEDOM TO ACT	38
IMPACT	10
KNOWLEDGE & SKILLS	118

Job Profile

No	Date	Profiler	Master	Description	Scored	Total Points
1	01/05/95	Analyst	Yes		Yes	516
2	11/01/93	Committee	No		Yes	536
3	11/01/93	Consultant	No		Yes	356
4	11/01/93	Supervisor	No		Yes	465

Questions   Score   Challenge   Master

Jobs

Table 3.15: *Framework: Adding or amending job profiles.*
This is the display where job profiles are added or amended. It tells you
what type of response is required (eg alphabetic, numeric). It allows very
quick analyses of profile changes by using the 'what if' function. Out of
range answers are flagged up by the system as data is entered.

Towers Perrin FRAMEWORK

File Edit Query Profile Report Window Help

ANALYST PROGRAMM   Database Demo 2.2

Questionnaire - IT43

Number	Question	Range	Response	Factor
1	Communicating Ideas	A - E	D	ACCOUNTABILITIES
2	Services & Advice	A - E	B	
3	Financial Resources	A - E	A	Subfactor
4	Physical Resources	A - D	A	Comm's - Ideas & Info
5A	Supervision of Staff	A - D	A	
5B	Number of Staff	A - F	B	Question Text
6A	Ad-hoc teams	A - C	B	How accountable are you for
6B	Number involved	A - F	A	communicating ideas and/or
7A	Contacts - Own Department	A - F	B	information?
7B	Contacts - Other Areas	A - F	B	
7C	Contacts - Trade Union	A - F	C	
8A	Contacts - Public	A - F	A	Type Alphabetic
8B	Conatcts - Artistes	A - F	A	
8C	Contacts - External suppliers	A - F	B	What If?
8D	Contacts - Pressure Groups	A - F	A	Points S-core
8E	Contacts - Regulatory Bodies	A - F	D	
9	Contacts - Press	A - F	B	Grade
10A	PS - Solution is Clear	A - D	B	
10B	PS - Well defined	A - D	B	
10C	PS - Influenced by precedent	A - D	A	OK Cancel

Job C: IT43, RE641, 10102, FN600, OP59, 18330, PA28, XY788

No: 1 01, 2 11, 3 11, 4 11

Questions

Table 3.16: *Framework: Actual and proposed salary structures.*
This is where actual and proposed salary structures can be entered.
Organisations can then produce graphs showing salary structure against best
fit line of job evaluation points and actual/market salaries. Also costing
reports can be produced showing the cost of bringing job-holders up to the
minumum of the proposed ranges.

Towers Perrin FRAMEWORK

File Edit View Query Window

Database Demo 2.2

Salary Ranges

Structure Operations

Grade Op 4

Range	Current	Proposed
Minimum	35000	
Upper Quartile	42000	
Maximum	45000	

Grades

Structure Operations

Name	Maximum Points	Salary Midpoint
Op 1	200	23001
Op 2	300	28501
Op 3	400	33001
Op 4	500	39001
Op 5	600	46001
Op 6	690	53501
Op 7	800	61001

Table 3.17: *Framework: Summary of total points.*
Shows some of the basic information held on jobs. Drop down menus
enable you to identify which division/department the job belongs to, which
salary structure to allocate the job to. Evaluated and actual information is
held to allow for the possibility of 'red circle' jobs

Towers Perrin FRAMEWORK

File   View   Window

ANALYST PROGRAMM   Database   Demo 2.2

Jobs

Total Points Summary

02/10/1998   Demo 2.2

Plan :   EBC   Total Points Summary

Code	Job Title	Profile	Evaluated Structure	Evaluated Grade	Division	Total	Factors
1833D	CHIEF EXECUTIVE	^ 1	Management	Mgt 5	Administration	922	
RE21	HEAD OF RESEARCH	^ 1	Management	Mgt 5	Development	877	
FN21	HEAD OF FINANCE	^ 1	Management	Mgt 5	Finance	850	
FA23	DIVISION CONTROLLER	^ 1	Management	Mgt 5	Administration	824	
PE21	HEAD OF PERSONNEL	^ 1	Management	Mgt 4	HR	761	
PA28	CHIEF PUBLICITY OFFICER	^ 1	Management	Mgt 4	Administration	748	
IT22	PROJECT MANAGER	^ 1	Management	Mgt 4	Development	727	
LE32	SOLICITOR	^ 1	Management	Mgt 4	Administration	668	
FN800	CHIEF ACCOUNTANT	^ 1	Management	Mgt 4	Finance	667	
PE33	PERSONNEL MANAGER	^ 1	Management	Mgt 4	HR	668	
FA29	SENIOR PREMISES MANAGER	^ 1	Management	Mgt 4	Administration	663	
PB38	SENIOR PUBLICITY OFFICER	^ 1	Management	Mgt 3	Sales	637	
XYZ8B	COMMUNICATIONS MGR	^ 1	Management	Mgt 3	Sales	639	
T625	EUROPEAN MANAGER	^ 1	Management	Mgt 3	Sales	687	
LE39	CONTRACTS MANAGER	^ 1	Management	Mgt 3	Administration	580	

3.4 EUROPEAN FACTOR PLAN (EFP), WATSON WYATT

Table 3.18: *Characteristics, factors/aspects of EFP*

Features	Characteristics	Factors/aspects
Know-how	■ *knowledge/skill*	■ *Job knowledge* – level of knowledge – complexity of knowledge – training and experience – specific qualifications for the job – specialist knowledge – keeping up to date/learning (3–6 levels) ■ *Business expertise* – level of knowledge – scope of knowledge – understanding of the company – knowledge of the market – language knowledge (3–6 levels)
	■ social skills	■ *Interpersonal contacts* – internal – external – contact with people within and outside the company – verbal communication skills – written communication skills – maintaining business relations – skills in negotiation and persuasion (3–7 levels)
	■ physical demands	■ *Eye-hand co-ordination* degree of eye-hand coordination (from 3 levels)
Problem solving	■ problem-solving capacity	■ *Type* of problems/situations ■ *Complexity* of problems/situations – type of problem situations – creativity and innovation – experience and tradition – nature of management received (3–6 levels)
Areas of responsibility	■ responsibility for business resources	■ *Nature* (sort) of responsibilities ■ *Scope* of responsibilities – responsibility for people – supervisory activities – type and scope of financial responsibility – monitoring standards and values (4–8 levels)
	■ influence on the company	■ *Nature* of influence ■ *Area* of influence – decision-making authority – decision level – time perspective – evaluation and management of business risks – type of influence on final results – area of influence on final results
Inconveniences	■ circumstances and physical demands	– possible *risks* (from three levels) – demands in respect of *travelling* (from three levels)

Specific system information

System technique

- Central to the EFP method is the allocation of values to 'factors' or aspects. As a result, a different 'weighting' per factor is obtained, which can be compared with assessment factors. The difference in the allocated 'weighting' per factor should, in the opinion of Watson Wyatt, be related to the strategic objectives of the organisation. By employing this approach, the system manager wishes to tailor the system to company-specific characteristics and developments, and to generate a job structure which closely reflects the internal relationships. This final point is achieved by Watson Wyatt by relating the 'weighting' per factor to the opinion/attitudes of local management.
- The method employs simple tables.

Procedures/implementation

- Watson Wyatt works with structured questionnaires, which relate to the factors of the method. These questionnaires are completed by the job-holders themselves. Answers are processed in the computer.
- The questionnaire is geared specifically to the characteristics of the organisation, and contains structured questions which can be answered by each job-holder. The questionnaires can be specifically prepared for each organisation component or job family.

Tools/computer support

- The answers from the questionnaires are processed in the computer, and checked for consistency.
- REWARD is the automated system employed by the system-holder, and consists of multiple modules. REWARD covers the entire procedure from job analysis through to market comparison and budgeting.

| Characteristics | Factors | Aspects |

Job knowledge

Definition:

Knowledge concerning job-related activities

Explanation:

This factor measures the demands imposed by the job in respect of knowledge concerning job-related tasks and activities. The factor is measured across a hierarchy of tasks, which ranges from the knowledge of tasks through to the 'theory and practice of more than one specialisation'. Within this factor, the subject area relates to 'technical skill or expertise', in so far as these aspects do not relate to 'business expertise'.

Table 3.19: *Classification table for job knowledge*

Level	Level definitions
1	The job requires knowledge of a limited number of tasks specific to the work of the unit/the team
2	
3	The job requires pure understanding of the principles and concepts relating to the job-holder's own area of knowledge/specialisation, and the practical knowledge of various related subject areas. This knowledge can be acquired by training or accruing considerable experience
4	
5	The job requires broad and extensive understanding of all or practically all job/subject areas relevant to the company

Business expertise

Definition:

Knowledge of the organisation, and the market in which the organisation operates

Explanation:

This factor measures the demand arising from the job in respect of knowledge concerning the organisation and the market in which the organisation operates. This knowledge is measured across a hierarchy of knowledge which ranges from knowledge of the job-holder's own department to knowledge of the overall business sector within which the organisation operates.

Table 3.20: *Classification table for business expertise*

Level	Level definitions
1	The job requires little knowledge of or understanding of the way in which the specifically allocated tasks relate to the work of the department, or the company as a whole
2	
3	The job requires a complete understanding of the way in which the own unit interacts with all or practically all other units, and how they support objectives within the company. The job also requires some understanding of the business sector within which the company operates
4	
5	
6	The job requires extensive understanding of the entire company and the business sectors, and a broad knowledge of other business sectors, including a complete understanding of economic, commercial and political questions which affect the business sector within which the company is active

Problem-solving capacity

Definition:

Analytical skills necessary for playing a specific role

Explanation:

This factor measures the problem level and the type of 'problem solution' required in the job.

Table 3.21: *Classification table for problem-solving capacity*

Level	Level definitions
1	The job consists of tasks and obligations, which may encompass the direct passing on of information. The job-holder employs specific techniques or methods for the implementation of tasks, and for solving clearly defined elementary problems. More complex problems are passed on to others
2	
3	The job covers an area of activities, which in the first instance require factual assessment, based on observation of the situation/analysis of the information. The problems may be identified by others, but in general further clarification is necessary before suitable action can be undertaken. The job-holder is expected to select the best possible solution for coping with the situation
4	
5	
6	The job requires the use of conceptual skills and vision, with a view to identifying crucial questions, ordering them according to priority, and anticipating problems, so that solutions can be offered. This calls for the use of increasingly abstract conceptual and intellectual skills, for developing and determining strategies, in an uncertain environment

Watson Wyatt, European Factor Plan EFP questionnaires

From the point of view of Watson Wyatt, the questionnaire occupies an important position in the collation of relevant job information and evaluation. The questionnaire replaces the traditional job description. Against this background, as examples, what follows are sections from the questionnaire as developed by Watson Wyatt for a specific organisation. An important point of departure in the EFP method is that the job-holder completes the questionnaire. After all, the job-holder is the best person to know about the actual content of the job. The information is processed using the computer programme REWARD, developed by Watson Wyatt.

The questionnaire starts with general information concerning the job, the job-holder, and a general introduction containing instructions for the use of the questionnaire. A detailed table of contents completes the start of this questionnaire.

The first question focuses on gaining an understanding of the primary objective of the job.

The general section then continues with use of time, which provides a picture of the time spent on the most important responsibilities.

Table 3.22: *Time spent on most important responsibilities*

Most important responsibilities	Estimate of time (to nearest 5%)	Main activities within each field
1	%	1
2	%	2
3	%	3
4	%	4
5	%	5
	= 100%	

Subsequently, an indication is given of the location within the organisation, in the form of an organisation chart, which provides horizontal and vertical line information. The following example gives an impression.

Table 3.23: *Sample organisation chart*

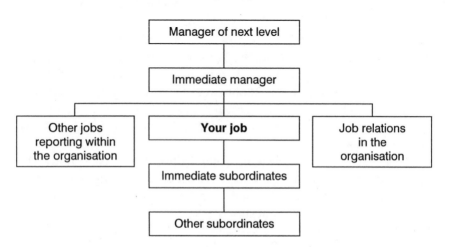

The questionnaire then deals with questions more specifically targeted at the various factors of the method. In this procedure, the model whereby explanation is given on the left, of the question which appears on the right of the form, is followed.

As already mentioned, the questions are harmonised with the automated processing procedure in the REWARD software program.

A. Knowledge and business expertise

A1. Education and experience

This section asks about the minimum knowledge necessary for the job. The knowledge can be acquired by various combinations of education, training and experience.

Official education stands for formal certificates. Experience in relation to the job stands for the total volume of *relevant* experience accrued within or outside the organisation.

Specific vocational qualifications necessary for the job are then listed.

Question:

> Circle one letter-number combination which relates most closely to your job; remember that the answer should represent the minimum job requirements, and not your personal profile.

When answering this question, use the following definitions:

Definitions:

Minimum required official knowledge: the normal level of basic education demanded in a recruitment advertisement.

Examples of the levels of education specified in A1 are:

– Level A: Junior General Secondary Education – Junior Secondary Vocational Education: Secondary Technical Education/ Junior Secondary Service Education

– Level B: Senior Secondary General Education – Senior Secondary Vocational Education: Senior Secondary Technical Education/ Senior Secondary Commercial Education

– Level C: Pre-university Education – Higher Vocational Education: Higher Technical Education/ Higher Commercial Education

– Level D: University graduate

– Level E: University post-graduate

Cumulative experience in relation to the job:

All experience (also accrued in previous jobs within or outside the organisation) necessary for functioning well in your current position.

Minimum required official education	Minimum cumulative experience in relation to the job					
	0–6 months required		From 1 to 2 years			More than 10 years
Basic skills in a number of practical subjects	A1	A2	A3	A4	A5	A6
	B1	B2	B3	B4	B5	B6
Ability in a technical subject at an advanced rate	C1	C2	C3	C4	C5	C6
Understanding of theories, principles and techniques in one or more technical, professional or academic fields	D1	D2	D3	D4	D5	D6
	E1	E2	E3	E4	E5	E6

A2. Specific qualifications for the job

Question a:

> Please mark any additional professional diplomas and/or certificates necessary for the job. Please differentiate between 'vital' (V) and 'desirable' (D) qualifications

Answer a:

	V	D
Tick only applicable boxes		

1. No vocational diplomas and/or certificates	1	☐	☐
2.	2	☐	☐
3.	3	☐	☐
4. Advanced management courses	4	☐	☐
5. Advanced technical vocational diplomas/certificates	5	☐	☐
6.	6	☐	☐
7. Specialist post-doctorate qualification	7	☐	☐
8. Membership of a professional association, if professionally desirable.	8	☐	☐
9.	9	☐	☐

A3. Specialist knowledge

This question deals with the specialist knowledge required for appointment to the job.

Question:

Please tick one box which best describes the minimum knowledge required within your job

Definitions:

General knowledge
– For jobs at this level, a general awareness of the basic principles of the subject area is required

Practical knowledge

Broad-based knowledge
– For jobs at this level, a factual understanding of the principles of the subject area is required, to enable the job-holder to apply this knowledge in the majority of situations

Extensive knowledge

Definitions:

> *Specialist fields* cover sections of subject areas or technical areas, for example:
> – production preparation
> – credit administration
> – salary administration
>
> A professional discipline covers a complete group of specialist fields or technical areas, such as:
> – financial management
> – human resources
> – information technology

Answer:

		Please tick only one box
1. General knowledge of one or more specialist fields and/or broad-based knowledge in the field of administration or service provision	1	☐
2.	2	☐
3. Broad-based knowledge of one or more specialist fields	3	☐
4.	4	☐
5. Extensive knowledge of one or more specialist fields	5	☐
6.	6	☐
7. Extensive knowledge of more than one professional discipline	7	☐

A4. Keeping up to date

This question deals with the rate at which and degree to which essential knowledge necessary for occupying this position is subject to change, and what resources are available within the job, for in-service training and updating specialist knowledge.

Question:

> Please tick the box which best describes the requirements for the job

Answer:

To keep up to date in the professional field	*Please tick only one box*	
1. Structural changes are dealt with during in-service courses, at work	1	☐
2.	2	☐
3.	3	☐
4. It is necessary to read and/or study regularly a wide range of journals, professional and technical information material, and to follow training courses	4	☐
5.	5	☐

A5. Understanding of own organisation

According to the question below, the following information is solicited: what degree of understanding of the various business activities within the job-holder's own organisation is required of the job-holder?

Question a: **Practical knowledge**

Question b: **Detailed understanding**

Definitions:

Practical knowledge means that you have a reasonable overview of the business processes, the procedures to be followed, and principles and questions which arise.

Detailed understanding means that you have a complete understanding of the business processes, procedures followed and principles/questions which arise.

World scale relates to the geographical region within which the organisation is active. For example, Europe is a world scale.

Below is a series of questions, set in the same manner as A1 to A4.

A6. *Knowledge of the market*
These questions relate to the level of 'market knowledge' required for fulfilling your job.

Question:

> According to the scales below, indicate the required depth and breadth of knowledge required. Depth indicates the level of knowledge and expertise intended. Breadth relates to the area or field of knowledge

Depth scale		Breadth scale
1. Not necessary	No knowledge required	1. Not applicable
2. General		2.
3. Practical	Sound understnding is necessary. This level of knowledge is used for solving day-to-day problems, and for responding to questions typical of daily practice, and makes the routine implementation of the job possible	3.
4. Broad		4. Knowledge of different elements within this category. Knowledge of all elements within the category
5. Extensive	Extensive understanding is required. This level of knowledge serves as a source of expertise for others within the organisation	5.

Answer

Depth (one type of knowledge)	Category	Breadth (various types of knowledge)
	Clients	
1 2 3 4 5	Local/national	1 2 3 4
1 2 3 4 5	International	1 2 3 4
	Competitors	
1 2 3 4 5	Local/national	1 2 3 4
1 2 3 4 5	International	1 2 3 4

Then follows a table concerning product knowledge.

A7. Language knowledge

B. Problem situations

The following questions relate to situations which may occur within your work. Problems should therefore be seen as problem situations which arise within your work.

Name three important problem situations in your job	Are there instructions or procedures for solving these problem situations?	
1	☐ yes	☐ no
2	☐ yes	☐ no
3	☐ yes	☐ no

If you ticked 'no': indicate in the table below what action you will take:

1. Consult with manager	For problem number 1 2 3
2. Consult with colleagues/ fellow employees	For problem number 1 2 3
3. Consult manuals	For problem number 1 2 3
4. Develop own solution	For problem number 1 2 3
	(circle the applicable number)

Explanatory note:

> In this section, the participant must be aware that, as in every organisation, the majority of tasks are extremely routine in nature

Definitions:

> 'Problems' within this context relate to questions, difficulties and highly demanding technical situations. (These need not necessarily be seen as negative.)

B1. Situation types

B2. Situation description

B3. Creativity and innovation
This question relates to ideas and improvements affecting products, techniques, services, procedures or policy areas within the organisation. The question asks whether it is necessary, in the job, to establish and/or introduce improvements or ideas.

Question:

> According to the relevant figures (1, 2), please indicate the answer which:
>   1 = is the most applicable
>   2 = is less applicable

Answer:

The job requires	1 = most applicable 2 = less applicable	
1.	1	☐
2. That I look for better methods for carrying out the work; however, I can normally introduce the majority of changes without approval from a senior employee	2	☐
3.	3	☐
4. The development and/or use of ideas from others for producing new knowledge, quality products/services, new markets, new techniques or new procedures/policy areas	4	☐
5.	5	☐

B4. Experience and tradition

B5. Nature of management received

C. Responsibility for company resources

D. Social skills

E. Physical demands and conditions

F. Influence

REWARD is the automated system, covering the entire procedure from job evaluation through the market comparison and budgeting.

The major system components are:

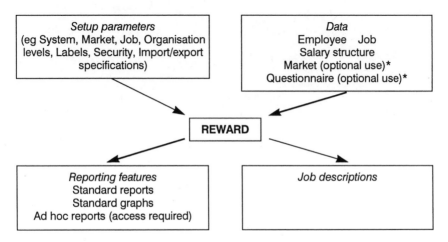

The Market Data module is a standard system feature. The term optional indicates that you can use the market-based or questionnaire-based job evaluation approach.

The following computer screens (see Tables 3.24 – 3.32) show how REWARD supports the EFP. In addition, note that like the approaches of other consultancies, REWARD provides an integrated system to link the results of job evaluation to:

■ data on employees;
■ information on remuneration, both at the level of the individual and at the level of pay policy;
■ compensation information, including history;
■ performance evaluation information;
■ information on market rates;
■ results of job evaluation.

The system opens with the main menu from which one of the above modules can be chosen. The following displays are restricted to the recording of the data from the job evaluation. After the opening display of EFP for each characteristic a separate display can be opened which gives entrance to the supporting displays (help displays) containing the definition of the table entries.

Table 3.24: *Main Menu*

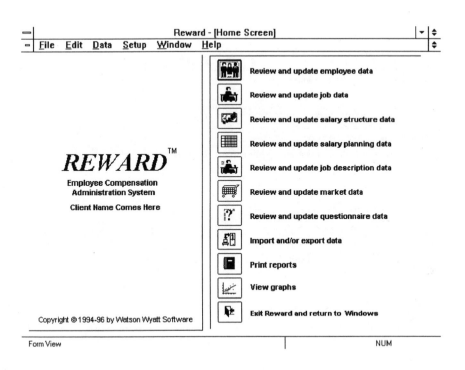

By choosing the number of the desired level the evaluation (scheme) is activated. As an example the supporting displays for the factors A (functional knowledge), D (problem solving) and G (interpersonal skills) are shown.

Table 3.25: *Selecting factors*

```
─|                    Reward - [EFP Short: Dummy 1, D01 NET]              ▼ | ⬍
─| File   Edit   Data   Setup   View   Format   Records   Window   Help      | ⬍
```

▶	▽	⊘	✚	▬	▣	⬆	🖹	🪳	■	♦?

Job Code	Qualifier	Region	Job Title		Case ID	Active?
D01		NET	Dummy 1			⬍ ☒

Eval Date	Eval Score	Eval Grade	Minimum	Midpoint	Maximum
25-Jul-96	100,00	1	F 24.000,00	F 30.000,00	F 36.000,00

▶ **European Factor Plan: Short Input Questionnaire**

(Click the letter proceeding the Factor to view the possible responses in detail)

A | █ ⬍ | Factor A: Functional Knowledge

B | 1. ⬍ | Factor B: Business Expertise

C | 1. ⬍ | Factor C: Leadership

D | 1. ⬍ | Factor D: Problem Solving

E | 1. ⬍ | Factor E: Nature of Impact

F | 1. ⬍ | Factor F: Area of Impact

G | 1. ⬍ | Factor G: Interpersonal Skills

EXAMPLE EFP - NO Q'AIRE

| ⏮ ◀ | Record: 1 | of 2 | ▶ ⏭ | |

Form View   NUM SCRL

Table 3.26: *Definition of aspects of factor A*
(functional knowledge)

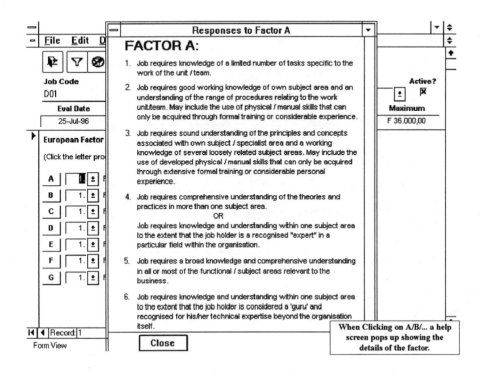

Table 3.27: *Definition of aspects of factor D (problem solving)*

| | Reward - [EFP Short: Dummy 1, D01 NET] | ▼ ◆ |

| File | Edit | D | Responses to Factor C | ▼ |

FACTOR D:

Job Code
D01

Eval Date
25-Jul-96

European Factor

(Click the letter proc

A	1. ±	F
B	1. ±	F
C	1. ±	F
D	■ ±	F
E	1. ±	F
F	1. ±	F
G	1. ±	F

1. The job consists of a number of straightforward tasks that require common sense and/or simple judgements.

2. The job works within well defined procedures which require selection of appropriate alternatives from defined options.

3. The job requires reasonable concentration and attention to detail in making judgements based on the analysis of factual information in straightforward situations.

4. The job covers a wide range of activities that require evaluative judgements based on the analysis of factual AND qualitative information in complicated and/or novel situations.

5. The job covers a wide range of activities that requires complex judgements based on advanced analytical thought. Problems will often call for an innovative approach, based on extensive research.

6. The job covers a wide range of diverse activities that requires judgements and solutions based on conceptual and on strategic vision and analysis.

Active?
± ☒

Maximum
F 36.000,00

Close

Another example

| ◄ ◄ Record: 1 | of 2 | ► ►| |

Form View

NUM SCRL

Table 3.28: *Evaluating job impact (areas of influence and time-scale)*

Reward - [Section B: Communication: Tech Contrib, 10 1 E]	▾	↕

File   Edit   Data   Setup   View   Format   Records   Window   Help

Job Code   **Qualifier**   **Region**   **Job Title**   **Case ID**   **Active?**

10   1   E   Tech Contrib   ☒

Eval Date   **Eval Score**

11-Jun-96   201

▶ **Section B: Communication**

B1: Level of internal contacts   **B2: Level of external contacts**

3. ±	Work group		1. ±	Customers
3. ±	Outside work group		2. ±	Suppliers
2. ±	Supv and Managers		2. ±	External professional contacts / advisors
3 ±	High level Managers		1. ±	Media / press

1.	Little or no contact with others			egulatory bodies
2.	Exchange and clarify routine information			
3.	Exchange and clarify complex information			other companies
4.	Advise/Persuade on day-to-day issues			
5.	Persuade/Negotiate on strategic issues			

Example of drop-down window

| ◀◀ ◀ Record: 1 | of 66 | ▶ ▶▶ | ← | | ➡ |

Form View   NUM   SCRL

Table 3.29: *Evaluating contacts*

—	Reward - [Section B: Communication: Tech Contrib, 10 1 E] ▼ ‡

Job Code   **Qualifier**   **Region**   **Job Title**   **Case ID**   **Active?**
10   1   E   Tech Contrib |_____| ‡   ☒

Eval Date   **Eval Score**

Errors

Error Type	Error Message
▶ Warning	140. Impact through expertise and influence of only a department (E1/E2)
Warning	124. Develop products, services etc. and influencing less than a function (D1/E2)
Warning	111. Planning and scheduling own work only and impact through the expertise provided (C4/E1)
Warning	110. Planning and scheduling own work only and requirement for analytical thinking (C4/D3)

Close   **Go To**   (Fatal Warnings Only)

Example of Logic checks
in the questionnaire

|◀ ◀ Record: 1   of 66   ▶ ▶| ◆

Form View   FLTR   NUM SCRL

Table 3.30: *Logic checks and reporting*

Reward - [Form: 2_Comp_Factor_B]											
<u>F</u>ile <u>E</u>dit <u>V</u>iew <u>R</u>ecords <u>W</u>indow <u>H</u>elp											

Section B : Comparison of Answers

	QUESTION B.1				QUESTION B.2					
	1	2	3	4	1	2	3	4	5	6
Accounting Assistant	2	2	1	1	1	1	1	1	1	1
Admin Supervisor	3	3	3	2	3	2	1	1	1	1
Controller	3	4	4	5	3	1	3	3	4	2
Exec. Secretary	2	2	2	2	2	2	2	2	2	2
IT Consultant	3	3	3	2	1	3	3	1	1	1
Jnr Test Engineer	3	3	2	1	1	1	1	1	1	1
Junior Secretary	3	3	2	1	1	1	1	1	1	1
Line Operator	2	2	1	1	1	1	1	1	1	1

Example of Question Comparison screen

Record: 1	of 8		

Form View   NUM SCRL

Table 3.31: *Comparison of answers*

	Knowledge	Communications	Planning & Organisation	Work Content	Job Impact	Physical Demands	
	Factor 1	Factor 2	Factor 3	Factor 4	Factor 5	Factor 6	TOTAL
Accounting Assistant	27	17	0	11	14	2	71
Admin Supervisor	50	31	31	89	85	2	288
Comodity Mgr.	113	46	50	54	55	2	320
Controller	174	76	94	89	176	2	611
DCEM	61	55	54	54	76	2	302
Entry Level Secretary	44	21	4	27	74	4	174
Finance Section Mgr	75	51	79	46	55	2	307

Reward - [Form: 1_Compare_Factors]

File Edit View Records Window Help

FACTOR COMPARISON

Record: 1 of 7

Form View

NUM SCRL

Table 3.32: *Comparison of job evaluations (report)*

Reward - [Section B: Communication: Tech Contrib, 10 1 E]	▼	↕

File	**Edit**	**Data**	**Setup**	**View**	**Format**	**Records**	**Window**	**Help**

Job Code	Qualifier	Region	Job Title		Case ID	Active?
10	1	E	Tech Contrib			☒

Eval Date	Eval Score
11-Jun-96	201

Section B: Communication

B1: Level of internal contacts

3.	Work group
3.	Outside work group
2.	Supv and Managers
⬛	High level Managers

1.	Little or no contact with others
2.	**Exchange and clarify routine information**
3.	Exchange and clarify complex information
4.	Advise/Persuade on day-to-day issues
5.	Persuade/Negotiate on strategic issues

B2: Level of external contacts

1.	Customers
2.	Suppliers
2.	External professional contacts / advisors
1.	Media / press

egulatory bodies

other companies

Example of drop-down window

⏮	◀	Record: 1	of 66	▶	⏭	◆		➡

Form View | NUM SCRL

In addition, REWARD includes modules for developing/adjusting a salary structure. Watson Wyatt calls this the Easy Salary Structure Analyses.

During the analyses these modules make it possible:

- to compare different salary structures;
- to compare an existing and a proposed salary structure;
- to adjust grades and salary ranges.

4

Salary structures

4.1 INTRODUCTION

The concept of 'pay' or remuneration consists of two elements: the pay policy and the technical instruments to design and implement this policy. The pay policy in its turn consists of the total packet of primary, secondary and tertiary benefits and other conditions of employment which constitute the (monetary) reward for the employee's performance.

The most important primary employment condition is defined by the salary structure of the organisation. That condition constitutes the main subject of this chapter. A salary structure is a coherent entity of figures (monetary amounts of salaries) which settles the individual pay according to fixed proportions (the salary scale) and determines the relationships in pay between jobs and job-holders within an organisational unit. The whole structure must be competitive to the environment (the external labour market) with which the organisation compares itself. These relations between salaries are determined by:

- the type of organisation with respect to both structure and culture;
- the competition in the labour market;
- the relationship between salaries and benefits;
- the extent of the scales (the desired difference/distance in pay between the highest and lowest jobs).

In determining salaries and salary structures an organisation needs to comply with the relevant laws and regulations. Examples of such regulations are the Equal Pay Act 1970, the Equal Pay (Amendment) Regulations 1983, the Treaty of Rome, Article 119, the EC Directives on Equal Pay and Equal Treatment, domestic case law and judgments in the European Court of Justice, as well as the Sex Discrimination Act 1975. Recently the EU Commission published *A code of Practice on the Implementation of Equal Pay for Work of Equal Value for Women and Men (COM96 336).*

Of course, the salary structure must comply with the law and regulations. In addition, it is sensible to take into account any possible changes in government. Until now the legislator has refrained from formally allowing, or regulating the influence of, or participation of workers' representatives in implementing job evaluation systems, pay policy and formal guarantees for the pay level of, for example, young employees. In other member states of the European Union such issues are usually regulated by law, which has important consequences for the entire remuneration process and for the roles of the various players. To illustrate this a summary of how such issues have been settled on the continent has been included in the Appendices. These may provide a starting point or a model for future negotiations between employers and workers' representatives and possibly government. These may also serve as examples of how to initiate and direct processes concerning the implementation of job evaluation methods and salary structures which are based on methods in an organisation. In this way a maximum degree of acceptance of the policy by employees would be ensured.

As is the case in several European countries, a future government might institute specific regulations on the remuneration of your employees. As a basis for pay negotiation in industries and individual organisations it could establish standards for the relationships between the pay of young employees and fully trained and mature employees. On the one hand such regulations may protect young employees against unfair treatment. On the other hand they may – within the context of government employment programmes – provide opportunities for young persons to enter employment because their salary levels are in accordance with their productivity. Such considerations are inspired by what is considered to be socially acceptable as well as by economic factors.

It will be obvious that the salary structure of a large retail chain will have a different design from that of a high-tech company. Also, local conditions may play a considerable role, especially at the level of operational jobs.

An insight into the existing salary structure can be obtained through a careful examination/analysis of:

■ the motives, constraints and circumstances that resulted in the present structure;
■ technical aspects such as: number of grades, slope of the salary curve, extent of the grades, relationships between minimum and maximum salaries, etc;

- characteristics of the structure, such as its rigidity or flexibility;
- the relationship between salary and benefits, between fixed and variable pay, between the weight of the function and pay. (See also discussion on the constraints of a pay policy in section 1.3.2 and the 'checklist on remuneration issues' at the end of the present chapter.)

The formal set-up of the salary structure, the salary scale, can best be illustrated by Figure 4.1. The rectangles represent the grades which constitute the total salary scale. The upward sloping line represents the primary relationship between the various grades as determined by the pay policy. The developmental stages within a salary structure are based on this basic figure.

To understand fully the meaning of the collective concept of a 'salary structure' the first part of this chapter will discuss the so-called traditional model. This model is the most common and is still included in quite a number of collective labour agreements.

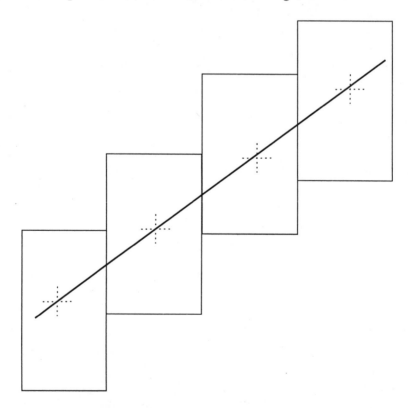

Figure 4.1 *The formal set-up of the salary structure*

Next, a number of variations will be examined which are primarily based on the 'open scales' model. But first we will discuss how the typical relationships within a grade are constructed.

The discussion will be supported and illustrated by graphs and figures which also refer to the same sample jobs in Chapter 2. In explaining the underlying techniques we need to refer to a number of mathematical and arithmetical concepts. Where necessary, these concepts will be explained in some detail. Extensive theoretical treatment of statistical and mathematical concepts are not included.

4.2 THE SET-UP OF A SALARY STRUCTURE

The traditional model is still the most common salary scale. This model will therefore be treated first as a basis for further discussions. Also we will examine how the sample jobs in Part I will behave within the various models.

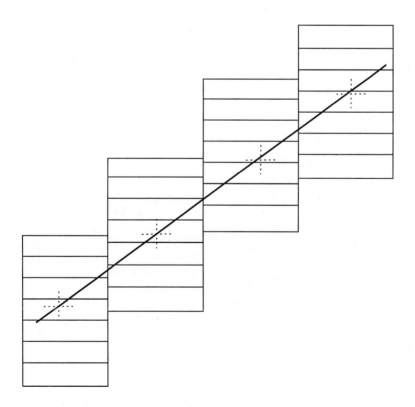

Figure 4.2 *The traditional model of a salary structure*

Two items characterise the traditional model (see Table 4.1):

- each grade has varying salary levels which depend on differences in the levels of the jobs;
- within each grade there are fixed amounts (steps) through which an employee progresses from the minimum to the maximum salary level.

The main features of this model are certainty and rigidity.

Table 4.1: Salary scale – traditional model

Grade	1	2	3	4	5	6	7	8	9	10	11	12	13	14
Step	£	£	£	£	£	£	£	£	£	£	£	£	£	£
0	10,526	11,789	12,907	13,968	14,722	16,637	18,797	19,910	21,187	24,154	27,533	31,661	36,408	41,870
1	10,819	12,115	13,258	14,376	15,178	17,155	19,382	20,573	22,094	25,186	28,709	33,014	37,968	43,661
2	11,112	12,442	13,608	14,789	15,638	17,674	19,968	21,235	23,002	26,222	29,890	34,373	39,528	45,456
3	11,405	12,768	13,963	15,197	16,099	18,192	20,558	21,898	23,909	27,254	31,070	35,731	41,088	47,251
4	11,698	13,099	14,314	15,610	16,560	18,715	21,144	22,565	24,816	28,291	32,251	37,085	42,648	49,046
5			14,669	16,018	17,021	19,234	21,730	23,227	25,723	29,328	33,432	38,443	44,208	50,842
6				16,430	17,482	19,752	22,320	23,890	26,630	30,360	34,608	39,802	45,768	52,632
7					17,942	20,270	22,906	24,557	27,538	31,397	35,789	41,155	47,328	54,427
8					18,403	20,794	23,582	25,219	28,445	32,429	36,970	42,514	48,888	56,222
9								25,882	29,352	33,466	38,150	43,872	50,448	58,018
10								26,549	30,264	34,502	39,331	45,230	52,013	59,813

A salary scale (see Table 4.1) is a (coherent) entity of amounts of salary that systematically settles the remuneration for the jobs to which this scale applies but note that not all functions in an organisation are governed by this salary structure. Exceptions are the salaries of executives and members of the board. In some industries high-level exempted functions are also excluded from the scheme. Other jobs may remain outside the scope of this regimen as well; examples of such jobs are jobs in the sales department. The remuneration of these jobs may consist of a basic salary supplemented by commission; the latter may even constitute the main part of the income. Jobs which may be difficult to fill through the labour market (as used to be the case in the field of automation) may receive salaries that deviate from the pay levels as stipulated by the salary scale. In the next section we will discuss the functions that are covered by the salary scale.

First we will explain some concepts by means of quantified examples from the salary structure in Table 4.1. This structure consists of 14 different grades. Each of these grades has a maximum and a minimum salary level. The difference between these amounts is called the *range* of the salary scale (pay range).

For grade 8 the pay range is £26,549 − £19,910 = £6,639, or 25 per cent of the maximum amount.

This difference is represented as a percentage of the maximum salary, because in order to use this difference correctly, it is convenient to take as a specific the maximum amount as a starting point. In this case the basic consideration is that:

> After some time every employee to whom the salary scale applies reaches the maximum salary level if the job is properly done. This maximum level is called the *maximum (standard) salary* or sometimes the *midpoint salary*

Expressing the relationships within a salary scale as a percentage of the maximum salary level (see Table 4.2) simplifies the adherence to these relationships. This percentage is part of the salary structure. That is, the *salary structure* determines in a technical sense the underlying relationships within the salary scale.

Each salary scale specifies the amounts of the consecutive pay rises. These amounts are called the *amounts of the salary scale. The steps of the scale*, however, are the serial numbers of the (fixed) amount of the increments as indicated in Table 4.1 in the column 'step' (0 to 10). This can be specified as follows.

The amount of the salary of grade 8, step 3 (8/3) is £21,898, the salary amount of 8/4 is £22,565, etc. The difference between consecutive steps is called an increment. In this example the increment amounts to £22,565 − £21,898 = £667. Over the scale small rounding-off differences may occur. An increment can also be expressed as a percentage of the maximum salary. In this case the difference is about 2.5 per cent.

If we take two consecutive grades it appears that the maximum salary of the one scale is higher than the minimum salary of the next grade. This difference is called *overlap*. If the maximum amount of grade 7 is £23,582 and the minimum amount of scale 8 is £19,910 then the overlap is £23,582 − £19,910 = £3,672. As a consequence, an employee who has reached grade 7 and is later on promoted to grade 8, has to be assigned to scale step 8/6 with a salary amount of £23,890, being the next higher amount in grade 8. If the employee had been given the minimum amount in grade 8, the promotion would have had an opposite effect of what was intended.

Finally there is the concept of *progression*. Progression refers to the difference between the maximum salary amounts within subsequent grades. The progression of the maximum amounts of scales 7 and 8 is (£26,549/£23,582) x 100 − 100 = 12.6 per cent. The difference between or progression of the minimum amounts is 6 per cent. The difference in progression between the minimum and the maximum amounts results from the difference in the number of steps within the scale (8 steps in scale 7 versus 10 in grade 8). The minimum salary as a percentage of the maximum salary is different in both scales (see Table 4.2).

Because the maximum and minimum amounts of the various grades are initially determined by the progression and only thereafter by the number of steps, small rounding-off differences may occur. The amounts of the steps in grade 8 vary between £138 and £139. This rounding off difference creates no practical problems.

In various industries and companies the maximum and minimum amounts of the salary structure can be fixed quite differently. The reasons for these limits are the nature of the work and the extent of the grade (for instance expressed in points taken from the job evaluation). Also the number of grades within a salary scale may vary. The organisation structure, culture, opinions of negotiating parties in the collective agreement and the (technical) knowledge of the personnel officer are factors which may influence these limits and provisions as well.

Supplementary to the technical structure of the traditional salary scale rules must be established in order to be able to apply the salary structure properly. These rules also co-determine the shape and structure of the salary scale.

4.3 APPLICATION OF THE SALARY STRUCTURE

After having explained the various elements of the salary scale, we will investigate the issues we may meet in applying the scale. By looking at the way in which salary structures are used in practice, the

Table 4.2: *Proportional relationship within the salary scheme*

Grade	1	2	3	4	5	6	7	8	9	10	11	12	13	14
Step														
0	90	90	88	85	80	80	80	75	70	70	70	70	70	70
1	92.5	92.5	90.4	87.5	82.5	82.5	82.5	77.5	73	73	73	73	73	73
2	95	95	92.8	90	85	85	85	80	76	76	76	76	76	76
3	97.5	97.5	95.2	92.5	87.5	87.5	87.5	82.5	79	79	79	79	79	79
4	100	100	97.6	95	90	90	90	85	82	82	82	82	82	82
5			100	97.5	92.5	92.5	92.5	87.5	85	85	85	85	85	85
6				100	95	95	95	90	88	88	88	88	88	88
7					97.5	97.5	97.5	92.5	91	91	91	91	91	91
8					100	100	100	95	94	94	94	94	94	94
9								97.5	97	97	97	97	97	97
10								100	100	100	100	100	100	100

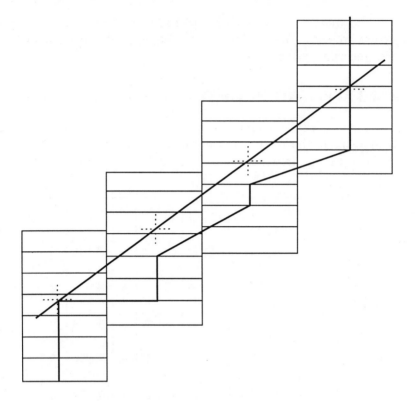

Figure 4.3:   *The traditional model of a salary structure*

concept is easily understandable. These variations have usually been constructed in response to the failing of the traditional model as an instrument to determine what is an adequate salary. The application aspects discussed in this section focus on the way in which:

– jobs are included in a salary scale;
– salaries develop within the rules of the salary structure.

The grade into which an employee is classified depends upon the grade in which the job has been assigned according to the methodology being used (usually a job evaluation method)

This sounds obvious and perhaps superfluous, but it is useful to differentiate between:

- the assignment of a job to a grade;
- the classification of an employee to a salary band.

This applies of course to all employees, especially in organisations in which job evaluation has been implemented. In these cases a job is assigned to a grade on the basis of the ranking of the job by means of a job evaluation method. The width of the various grades is expressed in points of the job evaluation point range, eg:

Grade	Grade width
1	0–50
2	51–70
3	71–90
4	91–110
etc.	etc.

For practical purposes the designation of the salary bands will be the same as that of the job grades, ie assigning a job to grade 1 will generally result in classifying the salary to band 1, etc. There might be reasons, however, to classify an employee in a grade that is different from the band to which his job has been assigned.

One of these reasons might be that a job or family of jobs receives a greater reward in the external labour market than would be allowed within the relevant grade. For years this has been the case for jobs in the field of automation and computers.

In determining the salary of a new employee the assignment of the job to a grade is obviously the first criterion to be looked at. However, if this employee is going to work in a job for which no job grade has been established, then the salary structure should give an indication as to a provisional classification of the employee in a band. In the traditional model this is done on the basis of:

– the experience of the new employee in similar work;
– the jobs immediately surrounding the new employee.

If a salary amount has been established for a specific job it will be increased to the next higher amount in the relevant salary band (see example below).

Grade	8
Salary band	8
Initially expected salary	£21,600
Next higher amount in the band	£21,898

By raising the 'initially expected salary' to the next higher 'salary scale', the employee can be certain of his position in the salary band and can follow the progress of his salary for himself. This method to determine a salary for a 'new' job is one of the most important reasons to continue to use the traditional model. In addition, the employee has been classified to a particular salary band.

For a large number of employees this settles the development of their salary. However, as jobs change as a result of the dynamics of the organisation or of the rapid technological developments an organisation experiences, an additional set of rules is required to determine the salaries of other employees. Also individual employees grow and acquire new skills and their developments may have to be reflected in their remuneration. Take the sample job of Head of Personnel from Chapter 2 and assume that his career progresses within the same organisation. As a young personnel manager he has been made responsible for a certain sector of the organisation and had to manage recruitment and selection of all personnel with the exception of the higher functions. The responsibility for the recruitment and selection of this latter group of employees in that period remained with the then Head of Personnel and Organisation. When entering employment the job was assigned to grade 9. Because the job-holder has only a few years' experience, he is offered a salary in grade 9 with 4 steps, amounting to £24,816. In time he has received the customary periodic increments. Not only has his experience gradually increased, but he has been allocated additional responsibilities. As a consequence, the job after being evaluated, is now assigned to grade 10. In this situation only the weight of the existing set of tasks has been increased, that is, that the job has not turned into a different, heavier one. Therefore this is called a re-evaluation of the job. It is quite justifiable for the job-holder to expect his salary to be adjusted accordingly. Various possibilities are open for such an adjustment:

– the salary is settled at the next higher amount in the new grade;
– first a periodic increment is offered according to the current grade, after which the final salary is fixed at the next higher amount in the new grade.

However, it should be kept in mind that a re-evaluation of the job has in fact already resulted in better prospects for the job-holder. In the new grade the employee can look forward to a higher maximum salary and this also constitutes a reward. Let us assume the first possibility. Suppose the 'old' salary corresponds with scale step 8 in grade 9 (9/8), then the salary amounts to £28,448. The new salary thus becomes £29,328 (10/5).

So far we have discussed what in general happens if, after a re-evaluation, a job is assigned to a higher grade. It can also happen that an employee is transferred to a totally different and heavier job. This kind of promotion can be within the same profession or to a new discipline or trade. Sticking to our example, let us suppose that the personnel manager, as successor to the Head of Personnel and Organisation, advances from grade 9/8 to grade 12, because it is clear to everyone that this job involves heavier responsibilities compared with the previous job.

In this case the promotion will not only consist of better prospects, but the job-holder will also be granted an increase in salary. The size of the difference depends on a number of factors besides the technical aspects of granting a rise. One such factor, for instance, is the relationship of the new salary to that of other, comparable jobs of, say, the controller. What will be decided depends very much upon the specific circumstances and therefore cannot be discussed here.

From a technical point of view and considering what may happen when a job is re-evaluated, the following rule or procedure may be carried out. The current salary is first increased by a periodic increment and then the job will be brought up to the new grade. In our example the salary is thus first raised from 9/8 to 9/9 (from £28,445 to £29,352). Then, the salary is fixed at the next higher amount in the new grade, or from 9/9 to 12/0 (from £29,352 to £31,661). By coincidence this is also the minimum salary of scale 12.

If we compare both possibilities the difference in the ultimate salary of the personnel manager is shown in Figure 4.4.

It is recommended that a specific date in the year is chosen in which salaries are adjusted, for instance 1 January or 1 July. The evaluation interviews will take place insofar as the results may influence the level of the salary adjustment. Re-evaluation or promotion may take place at a date different from the annual adjustment date. In this way it will not look as though a re-evaluation or a promotion is being offered exclusively for the sake of giving a rise. This situation may in particular occur when an employee has already reached the maximum of his present grade.

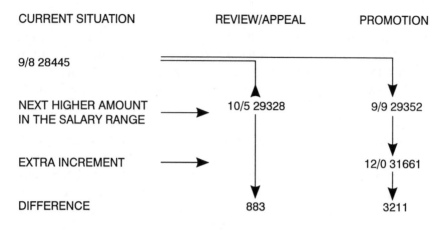

Figure 4.4: *Difference in salary increase after review/appeal and promotion*

After having pointed out all important aspects of the salary structure, in the next section we will discuss the technique of constructing a salary structure.

4.4 PARAMETERS OF A SALARY STRUCTURE

Earlier in this chapter we mentioned the factors which determine the interrelationships within a salary structure. These relationships can be expressed both in the form of nominal amounts and in percentages. The use of percentages is preferable, because they 'preserve' the relationships once they have been established. Aspects that determine the relationships within a salary structure are called the *parameters*. The construction of a salary structure is governed by the following parameters:

■ the slope of the pay policy line (or salary line);
■ a constant, or the starting point of the pay policy line on the Y-axis (at 0 on the X-axis);
■ the point range of the grade (sometimes called the width of the grade), usually expressed in points of the job evaluation;
■ the pay range of the grade, or the difference between the highest and the lowest amounts within the grade;
■ the number of grades.

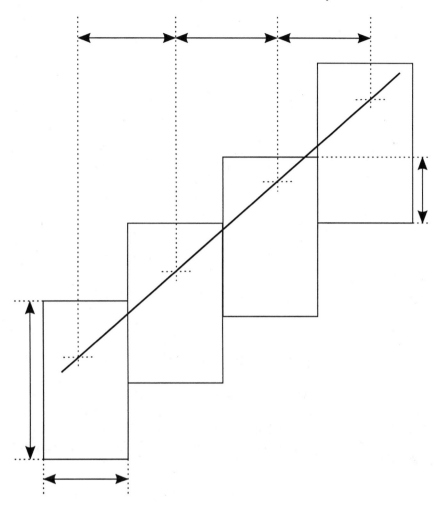

Figure 4.5: *The parameters of a salary structure*

The slope of the pay policy line is denoted by the letter a, the constant factor by the letter b. Thus, we can express the above graph by the formula:

S = a x P + b
S = amount of the salary;
a = factor for the slope;
P = points of job evaluation;
b = constant.

Figure 4.6 illustrates what the various parameters signify.

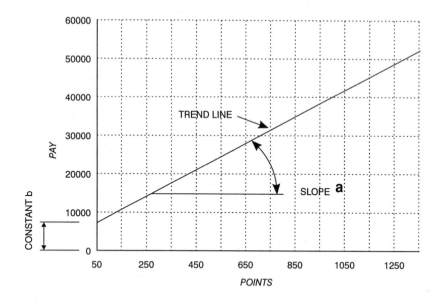

Figure 4.6: *Parameters, slope and intercept*

With this formula the salary corresponding with every point on the pay policy line or on the pay practice line can be calculated. The same basic formula is used in comparative analysis of salaries. It is therefore useful to know how to apply this formula when comparing the relationships of internal salary structure with the relationships in pay on the labour market.

The formula is also an important instrument when designing a salary structure. The number and width of the grades can simply be adjusted without influencing the position of the pay policy line. This is possible because every time the width of the grade has been adjusted for the points of the job evaluation, the middle of the scale can again be determined. Next the corresponding salary level can be calculated with the formula. Alternatively it is possible to express the middle of the scale in terms of job evaluation points for a particular salary level. Finally this formula is useful when calculating intermediate salaries if, for two points on a pay policy line, the evaluation points and their corresponding salaries are given.

The equation of the pay policy line is:

$$S = £34{,}909 \times P + £4364$$

If the scales are constructed as is shown on the X-axis of the graph, for the grade starting at 350 points and ending at 450 points, the amount of the middle of the scale (400 points) is:

$$S = £34,909 \times \frac{£350 + £450}{2} + £4364 = £18,360$$

In the case for any two points on the line, both the job evaluation score and the corresponding amounts are given, the general formula can also be used for determining the equation of a specific pay policy line. However, the procedure is more complicated. For example, suppose the corresponding salary level of 1,250 points is £48,000 and at 150 points the level is £9,600. The procedure is as follows.

The most important mathematical rule we have to observe here is that a positive number becomes negative and the other way round, if a number (here for instance £9,091) is transferred to the other term of the equation. If the two terms of an equation are both a negative number, then they can be changed into a positive number.

S	=	a	x P	+ b
£48,000	=	a	x £1,250	+ b
£ 9,600	=	a	x £ 150	+ b
————				—
£38,400	=	a	x £1,100	
£38,400	=	£34,909	x £1,100	

To determine b, the value of a we have just found (£34,909), is substituted in the formula:

£48,000	=	£34,909 x £1,250	+ b
£48,000	=	£43,636	+ b
£48,000 – £43,636 =		b	
£ 4,364 =		b	

Finally, it is possible that the pay policy line in Figure 4.6 is not straight but a curve. In that case the specialist can use logarithms and other mathematical operations to turn such curves into a straight line.

However, most personnel officers will have to take a somewhat more elaborate route that is equally effective. Every curve can be seen as being composed of small sections that are straight. For each of these sections the above mathematical operation can be applied to reduce the issue into more manageable proportions.

Skills for using logarithms and comparable mathematical techniques are an advantage. However if these are applied to 'straighten' curves, the usefulness is considerably reduced.

The next two parameters of the salary structure are the pay range and the width of the grade and its corresponding midpoint. These are illustrated in Figure 4.7.

In determining the position of the grade (width) in relation to the pay policy line, the middle of the grade expressed in evaluation points is usually the best starting point from a technical point of view. Also the position of the width of the range of a grade, or pay range, is important. It is therefore necessary to define the so-called midpoint of the grade as follows:

The midpoint of a grade is determined by:
- the salary level that can be reached by any employee who performs his job 'normally'; and
- the middle of the grade calculated on the basis of the upper and lower limits of its evaluation points

---

'Normal performance' is taken to be: carrying out the job in such a way that the results comply with predetermined qualitative and quantitative requirements, taking into account the demands concerning accountabilities, competencies and suchlike, which have been laid down in the job description.

In the following section the midpoint is in each case the starting point for the internal relationships of a salary structure. For example, the minimum and the maximum salary of a grade will be represented as a percentage of the midpoint (= 100 per cent) of the grade.

Other aspects of the pay policy that can be linked directly to the salary amount are in practice also conveniently expressed in relation to the midpoint. Particularly in so-called open scale systems these ratios to the midpoint are a major feature.

4.5 MORE THAN ONE JOB EVALUATION METHOD

An additional complication may occur when an organisation employs more than one job evaluation method to differentiate between blue and white collar jobs. The job of Head of Personnel may thus be evaluated through the Hay method, while the job of secretary is weighted by means of Framework. In such a case, however, it is virtually

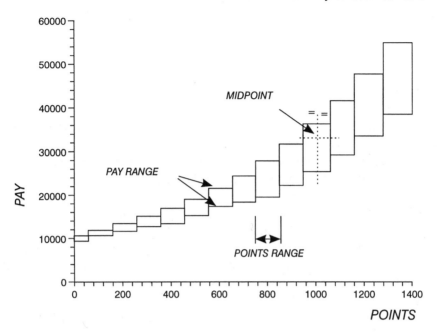

Figure 4.7: *The parameters: grade width and pay range*

impossible to compare the resulting scores of the evaluation of jobs according to these different methods.

As a general rule, comparing results of different job evaluation methods should be restricted to a particular organisation or at least to the same line of business. The use of more than one job evaluation method sometimes creates problems in the border area between both methods. These problems can frequently be solved by evaluating jobs in these border areas with both methods to establish a final score for each method. The border area needs to be taken widely enough to allow statistical calculations which provide a sound and acceptable basis for comparisons within a specific organisation. In addition, it is important to check whether the score structure of the various charac-teristics of the method and in particular the chosen entries to the tables, do not provide incompatible or conflicting outcomes.

Suppose the sample job of Secretary is classified in method 'A' for the characteristic 'know-how' at the level of 'general knowledge'. Such a result is incompatible with a score for the same characteristic at the level of 'professional know-how' if this job has been evaluated to according to method B. Differences like this are not entirely fictitious. They occur in practice, because in translating the 'characteristics' of the various methods in their respective 'factors/aspects', jobs might have been interpreted or perceived differently.

Comparing results from various job evaluation methods thus involves more than matching total scores. If an organisation does not possess sufficient expertise in this field, it should discuss the issue with both system-holders in order to work out a satisfactory conversion formula.

Another problem which will be encountered when using two methods is the difference in the width of salary ranges. If one method uses geometrical scales and the other arithmetical scales, then the same score on both salary ranges produces different salaries. This makes the scales incompatible, because 20 points on a geometrical series have an entirely different meaning from 20 points on an arithmetical series. This is why in the Hay method differences of 20 job evaluation points between lower jobs signifies another relationship than 20 job evaluation points between two jobs higher in the hierarchy. In the Hay method, differences are expressed as percentages using the following definitions:

---

15 per cent = 1 step (just noticeable difference)
30 per cent = 2 steps (a clearly noticeable difference)
45 per cent = 3 steps (a quite evident difference)

4.6 IMPLEMENTING A PAY POLICY

In order to determine the number of grades a careful consideration is required of the way in which the pay policy of an organisation is being implemented. Two instruments are available:

1. the jobs ranking list (see Table 4.3);
2. the scatter diagram (see Figure 4.9).

The jobs ranking list shows all jobs in the ascending order of their weight, expressed in job evaluation points. The list provides an initial picture of their relative differences or the relative similarity or equivalence. However, the jobs ranking list lacks a second dimension: the salary actually paid. The relationship between job evaluation score and salary is usually expressed in a so-called scatter diagram.

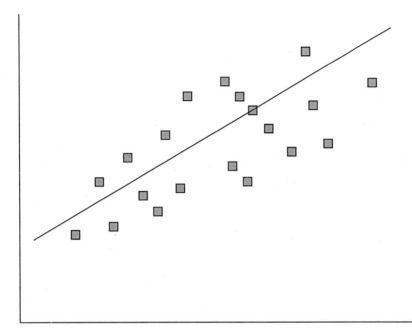

Figure 4.8: *Shape of the pay practice line*

Table 4.3 *Jobs ranking list*

Job evaluation points	Jobs
45	Cleaner
51	Post man
63	Driver
68	Typist
70	Receptionist
85	Department secretary
89	Switchboard operator/receptionist
105	Computer operator
121	Head of post room
136	Secretary
148	Calculator/cost accountant
159	Programmer
165	Payroll/personnel administrator
193	Head of accounting
201	Marketing assistant
203	Sales representative
235	Systems manager
etc.	etc.

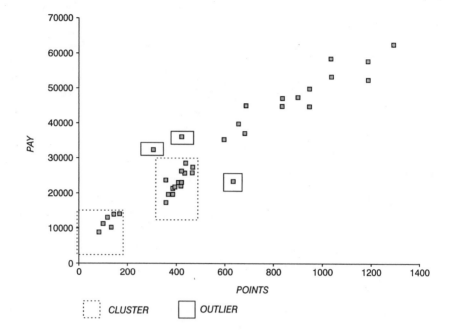

Figure 4.9: *The scatter diagram: clusters of job scores and deviations*

From the jobs ranking list and the scatter diagram 'problem cases' or deviations ('outliers') from the 'ordinary' pattern become apparent. Also, concentration of jobs in a particular area (clusters) are immediately noticed. If a regression line is calculated and a maximum and minimum line are drawn without taking into account salaries which deviate from the pay policy line, we obtain a graph as illustrated in Figure 4.10.

For several reasons the specific salary amount or level will not be calculated for every job with an 'own' score including:

- the results of the job evaluation are not conclusive on the level of the function. It should be kept in mind that the job evaluation results are but a (systematised) assessment of the level of jobs within acceptable limits;
- small differences in job level are not felt by the job-holders to such a degree that a difference in pay is warranted;
- the level of the job is not the only determining factor of the salary;
- from an administrative point of view it is very cumbersome and time consuming, especially in larger organisations, to monitor the development of the individual pay separately for each job.

Clusters of jobs which appear in practice demonstrate that the score of the job evaluation has only a limited effect on smaller salary differences.

If we try to differentiate the pay of jobs, we have to realise that in lower jobs a small difference in the weight of a job is felt sooner than in higher ones. Consequently, for the positions lower in the hierarchy, relatively small grades (in terms of job evaluation points) will be designed while those for higher positions will be relatively wider. But the points are not the only factors which determine the level of the salary in the design of a new structure.

Another important factor is the pay level in the labour market to which the organisation wants to attune its pay policy. In general it may approach a number of consultancy firms (see Chapter 5). Alternatively it may carry out its own investigation. The advantage of the latter approach is that the organisation can select its own partners for participation in such a study. In exchange for their co-operation these partners usually demand access to the results of the investigation. And that usually creates problems. Not every Personnel Department is able to perform a technically sound analysis of the pay

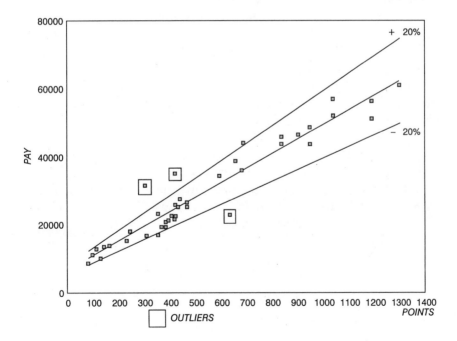

Figure 4.10: *The scatter diagram: individual job scores within a band of +/- 20 per cent*

in the labour market. Chapter 5 will provide some assistance in choosing the most appropriate approach. It is also recommended that the parameters and constraints for such a salary study are carefully considered in advance. Only then will the comparative study be really useful and deliver results which can serve as a basis for comparison in any subsequent studies.

When collecting external information, the organisation should not restrict itself to the general picture of the labour market. The information obtained must be of such detail and structured in such a way that it provides insight into the relationships in pay of different job families and individual jobs. The scarcity of computer personnel a few years ago caused a substantial increase in salary for these jobs. If in assessing the labour market we do not take into account the effects of these or similar conditions, we may in the end draw the wrong conclusions. When formulating pay policy we may set the salaries at too high a level and thus increase costs unnecessarily.

Differences in pay levels on the labour market and those within the salary structure of an organisation are not only the result of differences between and within job families, but are also caused by regional influences, differences between higher and lower jobs, differences in lines of business, differences in sales, etc. Consequently, an organisation should be careful in testing its policy against external information.

An additional problem is caused by 'mistakes' of the organisation in the past. Choosing a salary structure implies choices concerning individual deviations and exceptions. If these individual issues and considerations are not or cannot be incorporated in the salary structure, a solution must be found in the rules for applying the structure. In many cases, during the implementation of a new salary structure some guarantees and other provisions have been developed. These contain procedures for settling individual salaries.

Which factors determine the competitive position of an organisation on the labour market? A first indication is its own pay policy, because this reflects factors such as:

— age structure;
— years in employment;
— expectations and prospects, whether or not linked to career expectations;
— attractiveness of the organisation to new employees;
— relationships between pay, benefits and other terms of employment.

Another indication is whether the organisation has labour-intensive or capital-intensive business processes. If these questions have been duly answered, establishing the level of the pay policy line (the line connecting the midpoints, see Figure 4.7) can be started. In addition the pay policy line is an instrument for making comparisons with the labour market in the future, independent of the precise design of the salary structure.

The next parameters determine the basic design of the salary structure (they were discussed earlier; see Figures 4.6 and 4.7):

- salary band (pay range);
- width of job grade (points range);
- the midpoint;
- the number of job grades or salary scales;
- the slope of the pay policy line;
- the distribution of the observed salaries in the scatter diagram (see Figure 4.9).

Next these parameters are influenced by the following internal elements:

- The difference between the highest and the lowest score of evaluation points – points A and B in Figure 4.11 – and the number of grades. This influences the width of the range.
- The difference in salary at:
  - the highest and lowest score A – B;
  - highest and lowest observed clusters D – E; this influences the slope of the pay policy line;
- Finally we assess the difference between the salary actually paid at the highest and the lowest score/cluster as the basis for determining the salary range.

Establishing the *width of the salary range* is the first step in developing a salary structure. The salary ranges have been invented, because it is not very practical to determine a salary for each job evaluation point, though some companies do. They use a formula in which the number of job evaluation points are a variable (see the formula for calculating the pay policy line). The result is a salary and a salary range for that score.

In order to determine the width of a salary range an analysis of Figure 4.11 should be made. It is necessary to define clusters of jobs which are more or less equivalent judging by their total score.

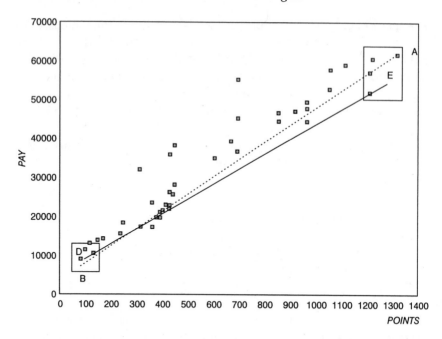

Figure 4.11: *Connecting the highest and the lowest salary levels*

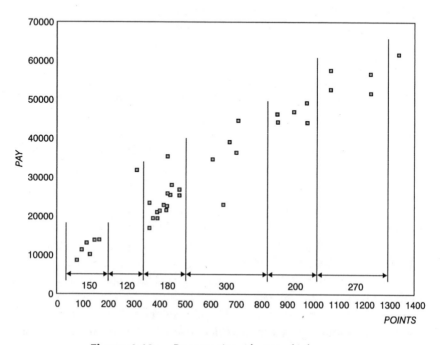

Figure 4.12: *Pay practice, cluster of job scores*

At first this causes a less regular definition of the width of the grades (see Figure 4.12). We call the series of grades regular, if the distances between different grades, measured nominally, proportionally or otherwise, follow a smooth course (Figure 4.13).

It will be clear that the spread as given in Figure 4.12 is not satisfactory and that a different distribution is needed. And because the scores on the X-axis have been determined according to the Hay method, it is obvious to look for a distribution using percentages.

The points range is set at 20 per cent difference.

An important consideration in determining the range of the grades is the number of steps an employee goes through. In addition, it should be established whether all grades need to have the same number of steps. The number of steps in a scale reflects, amongst other things, the number of years of employment insofar as they influence the execution of the job (increasing experience). Another consideration is the average ages at which employees start in a job and leave it. For the lower grades the starting age may be fixed at 23 years and for higher grades at a somewhat higher age. The setting of the maximum age is determined by:

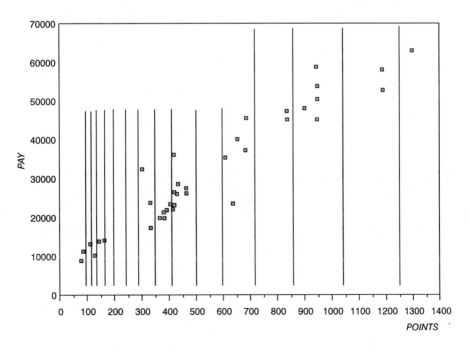
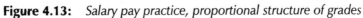

Figure 4.13: *Salary pay practice, proportional structure of grades*

 - external information, which may have been obtained from:
   - comparative studies of salaries;
   - common practice in labour agreements;
 - the wishes of the organisation.

Arguments must be carefully weighed, they must also take into account collective labour agreements, general opinions and attitudes in society, the relationships between gross and net salaries, and between lower and higher incomes, and the pay policy and practice in the organisation. The latter point is important, because the levels of individual salaries are not set in a vacuum or left to chance. It is therefore recommended that existing practices are carefully analysed and weighed against the other consideration. Again, external information plays an important role.

What are the core jobs in an organisation? Let us take again the imaginary company Fiction Publishing Limited from Chapter 2 as an example. From the business characteristics it appears that the job of Head of the Publishing Group must be a core job which comes close to the very rationale of the organisation. Thus it is important to study the market in order to obtain a picture of the pay level for this type of job. Though this is a core job to this organisation, it does not imply that the job will have to be rewarded at a higher or lower rate than that currently in the market. The benchmark should be what is being paid for similar jobs in the market or for comparable jobs in other industries.

Another important aspect is the difference between basic salary and the so-called total cash. In other words, which variable salary component should be added to the basic pay to arrive at a total amount of income. This issue will be discussed in some detail in Chapter 5.

If a clear picture of all these relationships has been obtained, we can proceed to designing the outlines of the salary structure, more in particular the range and the width of the various grades as well as the number of grades and the slope of the pay policy line. We are thus back at the main issues of the traditional salary scale which we discussed at the beginning of this chapter. All aspects and elements of the construction of the traditional salary scale have now been discussed, with the exception of the steps of the scale (see Figure 4.14).

The size of the steps of a grade may follow a linear course or a non-linear one. This means that in the former case the (periodic)

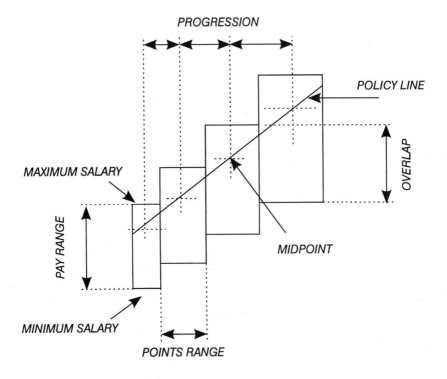

Figure 4.14: *Parameters for a salary structure*

increments within the grade are all equal, while in the latter the increment will decrease in practice.

If we take grades 11, 12, 13 and 14 from the traditional salary scale in Table 4.1 as examples, we can compose a Table (4.4) which quantifies the parameters from Figure 4.14.

As we have seen before, the construction of a grade is closely linked to the pay practice of the organisation (individual scores and the corresponding salaries). Certainly if we have to deal with bigger populations it may require a lot of effort and sorting out to construct optimum grades on the basis of these individual scores and salaries.

Table 4.4: *The parameters of a salary scale*

Salary scale	Point range	Minimum salary	%*	Maximum salary	Progression	Overlap
3	75–90	12907	88	14669		701
4	91–108	13968	85	16430	12	1708
5	109–130	14722	80	18403	12	1766
6	131–156	16637	80	20794	13	
11	500–600	27533	70	39331		7670
12	601–720	31661	70	45230	15	8822
13	721–864	36408	70	52013	15	10143
14	865–1037	41870	70	59813	15	

4.7 PERFORMANCE-RELATED PAY

Some pay elements are variable, such as profit-sharing, gain-sharing, bonuses, incentives, premiums and, of course, performance-related pay. Of these, performance-related pay in particular is of an individual nature and is usually expressed as a proportion of the total amount of the salary. It is sometimes so obviously linked to the salary scale that the possibilities can be read directly from the scale. In other cases the performance-related pay is expressed as a percentage of the salary according to the scale. Both versions will be discussed.

If an organisation wants to implement performance-related pay the functioning of employees needs to be assessed. In Part I we have stressed the importance of a proper job description; elsewhere the subject of assessing, and assessment and appraisal systems have been extensively discussed. Within the scope of this book it will be sufficient to point out a number of preconditions which any job evaluation system at least must satisfy. 'In any system of performance-related pay it should be established to what extent the employee has succeeded in accomplishing his tasks in the previous period.' For this purpose other evaluation methods and approaches may be used, such as performance measurement and assessing the potential of employees.

The results of the assessment of the performance of individual employees has to be translated into a monetary reward. In most assessment systems an individual is assigned to one level of performance from a series which corresponds with a certain percentage.

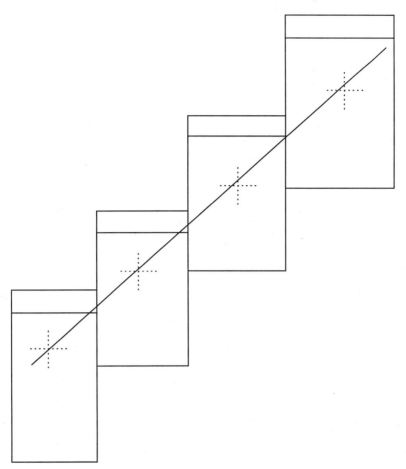

Figure 4.15: *Set-up of performance-related pay*

Example:

0 per cent – a *normal* performance; the employee meets all requirements of the job

2 per cent – the employee performs *recognisably* better than might have been expected under normal conditions

4 per cent – the performance is *clearly of a recognisably* higher level than might have been expected from the employee under normal conditions

7 per cent per cent – the employee performs *exceedingly well*

10 per cent – the employee performs *outstandingly well in all respects*

The terms which are used as criteria should be defined as precisely as possible and must also be perceived in the organisation as clearly distinct. 'Insufficient performance' or similar terms should not be used in an assessment system, because performance-related pay is meant to reward achievements and not to establish whether a person has performed insufficiently. In that case a job evaluation would be more appropriate.

Apart from a so-called 5-point scale as in the example, in a number of cases it may be sufficient to use a 3-point scale. Refinements resulting in a 7-point scale or more bear the risk that the assessment uses more subtle distinctions than the employees in practice perceive as real reflections of differences in performance. In that case the system will overshoot its mark, as the system itself is clearly regarded as more important than its objective: rewarding superior performance. Therefore, a 3-point scale is preferable.

The different percentages – in the example 0, 2, 4, 7 and 10 per cent – should also be chosen so that they are in accordance with the other relationships within the pay policy. The most obvious solution is to link the percentages to the successive maximum amounts, ie the progression in the salary structure. In some cases the highest percentage of the performance bonus will be higher than the percentage of the progression. Other relationships are in use as well. The 10 per cent performance bonus in the example is lower than the progression percentage of the pay policy line in Table 4.6. A clear distinction in the definitions of 'steps' is important, because that determines to a large extent whether the differences in pay will be accepted and appreciated. In other words, the overlap between consecutive salary bands should be carefully taken into account.

The percentages in the example can be incorporated in a separate salary scale. Each grade from the salary structure is divided into five columns (see Table 4.5). To compare the percentages of the performance bonus with the salary level, an additional column provides grade 12 at a 0 per cent performance bonus.

Table 4.5: *Amounts of salaries in grade 11 at separate performance levels*

Scale step	11					12
	0%	2%	4%	7%	10%	0%
0	27,533	28,085	28,637	29,462	30,288	31,661
1	28,709	29,285	29,861	30,720	31,579	33,014
2	29,890	30,490	31,090	31,982	32,880	34,373
3	31,070	31,694	32,314	33,245	34,176	35,731
4	32,251	32,899	33,542	34,507	35,477	37,085
5	33,432	34,104	34,771	35,774	36,778	38,443
6	34,608	35,304	35,995	37,032	38,069	39,802
7	35,789	36,509	37,224	38,294	39,370	41,155
8	36,970	37,709	38,448	39,557	40,666	42,514
9	38,150	38,914	39,677	40,819	41,966	43,872
10	39,331	40,118	40,906	42,086	43,262	45,230

In such performance-related pay systems careful consideration should be paid to the rules which will be applied if the performance level of an employee falls back. Answering the following questions may help:

– Should the salary of the employee be an amount that can be found in the salary scale?
– If the salary must be an amount that is included in the scale, how will the new salary be calculated?
– How will the next increments be determined if the amount of the salary does not need to be included in the scale?
– What are the consequences for the pension entitlements of the employee?

In the next section we will discuss a version that deals with these issues.

4.8 PRECONDITIONS FOR A NEW SALARY STRUCTURE

The traditional pay system is quite rigid in its structure and consequently in its use in practice. Companies with a strongly regulated production process in which a large number of different bonuses and allowances are used, eg for unpleasant work, will think that approach quite appropriate, because it offers some certainty. An employee can usually determine for himself what his salary, after the next rise or pay round, will be.

If an organisation wants a more flexible form of performance-related pay which puts a greater responsibility with the managers (of a department), it must adopt or develop another approach. In the following example the flexible system described need not be the only conceivable solution: other solutions are also feasible. We just want to provide an example of how an existing, rigid system can be changed into a flexible one at relatively low costs.

Preconditions of a new system

Before starting the development of a new system it is recommended that some preconditions are formulated which the new system will have to meet. For instance, the pay system to be developed in section 4.9 will have to meet the following requirements:

---

a. The new pay system should not create too many obstacles for adapting individual salaries

b. The costs of classifying a salary should be kept to a minimum, ie a change in salary must not cause higher costs than strictly intended

c. If the reasons for granting a performance-related allowance cease to exist, that allowance must be terminated

d. In creating a pay system or granting a performance-related bonus, the consequences for other benefit entitlements should be taken into consideration

e. Performance-related bonuses must be linked to the time period over which the performance is 'measured' and the nature of the performance

f. Granting a performance-related bonus must be founded upon an assessment of the way in which the employee functions

---

Note: The above preconditions may differ in each organisation. They are intended as a starting point for developing a flexible salary structure in the next section.

4.9 TOWARDS A FLEXIBLE SALARY STRUCTURE

One way to break through the rigidity of the strict steps mechanism of the traditional pay system, is the so-called open scales system. In principle an *open scales system* comprises three elements for each grade:

1. a minimum salary;
2. a maximum salary;
3. an average increment.

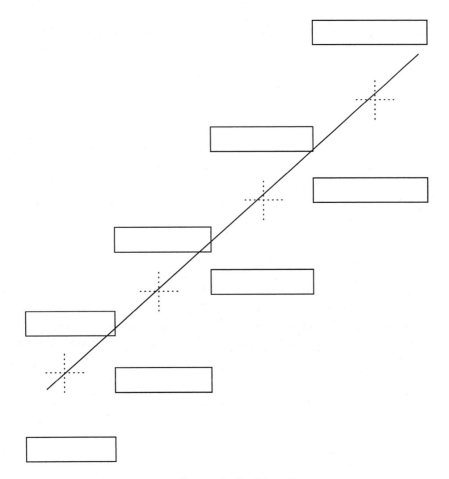

Figure 4.16: *Shape of a flexible salary structure*

To illustrate this, these elements for grade 10 of the open scales system are as follows:

Minimum salary	£24,154
Maximum salary	£34,502
Average increment	£1,035

One of the advantages of the open scales system is that it is irrelevant whether or not the difference between minimum and maximum salary is an exact multiple of the average increment. For instance in the case of scale 10 (£34,502–£24,154)/£1,035 = £9,998 and thus not exactly equal to 10 scale steps. The minimum and maximum salary in the open scales system have the same function as in the traditional system. In the traditional pay system the size of a (periodic) increment may vary not only between the grades, but also within an individual scale. In the open scales system for each scale a specific increment is set, which we will call the *average increment*.

> A characteristic of the open scales system is that any amount between the minimum and maximum salary of a scale is acceptable to the system

Thus, in the example, any amount between £24,154 and £34,502 may be taken as a step of the scale.

In accordance with the precondition mentioned in section 4.8 the open scales system accepts:

– any salary amount for a newly appointed employee;
– any reassignment of a job to another grade without entailing an unintended adjustment (increase) of the amount of the salary;
– any adjustment of the pay (policy) line, ie the pay level of the organisation in relation to that in the labour market (usually the maximum pay line of the organisation), without any consequences for the individual salaries;
– any (periodical) increment expressed as a percentage of the average increment.

There needs to be a provision for adapting a salary in case a job is re-evaluated or a promotion is awarded. This can be done, for instance, by setting a percentage of the difference between the maximum salaries of the relevant (or successive) grades. It is also possible to express the salary adjustment as a percentage of the average increment of the new grade.

In implementing an open scales system it is recommended that consideration be given as to whether or not limits should be set to salary increments. This seems to be a return to the rigidity of the traditional system, but this provision is intended to prevent relatively large differences in increments from being set. In addition, it is recommended that each periodical increment that deviates negatively or positively from the average increment should be explained to the employee in writing.

Other factors as well may make it necessary or desirable for an employee to progress fast through the salary scale. One of the most important reasons is the situation on the labour market. It may occur that an employee has been taken on at a higher salary than his new colleague. The incumbent employee may feel that to be an injustice, which could be an inducement for this employee speedily to catch up his arrears in salary. In this way the 'equal pay' situation within the organisation or unit is restored.

Looking back on what has been said on the open scales system so far, it appears that it fulfils two of the preconditions because:

– a transfer of a job to a different grade is possible without the system enforcing an adaptation of the salary (precondition a);
– any (new) salary that fits in between the minimum and maximum salary of the grade is acceptable to the system (precondition b).

Adapting the pay policy to changing conditions is simpler now, though the organisation has to take care that individual salaries are equal to or higher than the minimum salary of the salary scale concerned (see Figure 4.17).

4.10 RELATIVE SALARY POSITION: THE COMPA RATIO

It creates a disadvantage if a salary structure has no fixed salary steps within each salary scale. Because the employee cannot trace his individual salary in the scale, he is unable to check whether the salary adjustment granted to him is in accordance with the principles of the pay system. In practice it appears that individuals in higher positions also have difficulties in forming a proper opinion on a salary adjustment which they have received, particularly if this adjustment consists of several components, as in the case of a complete review of

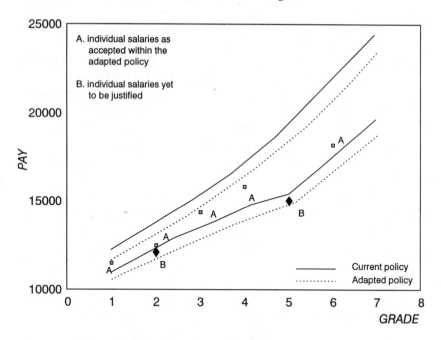

Figure 4.17:   *Adapting the salary policy line in an 'open structure': effect on individual pay.*

the salary which comprises a general and an initial increment. Some explanation is then certainly due.

Management and the Head of the Personnel Department need more insight and must have a proper understanding of the relationships between pay policy and pay practice. An extremely useful instrument for this understanding is the concept of the relative salary position, which we call the CompaRatio. This CompaRatio is calculated by expressing the individual salary as a percentage of the maximum (standard) salary (midpoint) of the grade concerned:

$$\text{CompaRatio} = \frac{\text{Actual salary}}{\text{Midpoint salary}} * 100$$

The relative position of a job in relation to other jobs and salaries is visualised independently of grades. In addition, an individual CompaRatio can be compared with the CompaRatio of the department of the entire organisation. For instance, substitution of the 'salary' in the formula by the sum of the individual (full-time) salaries and the 'maximum (standard) salary' by the sum of the maximum (standard) salary of each employee of the department or organisation gives the CompaRatio of the chosen entity to which the individual employees belong. Table 4.6 calculates the CompaRatio for part of the salary scale discussed at the beginning of the chapter (Table 4.1).

Table 4.6: *Example of an open scale structure*

Grade	4	5	6	7	8	9
Minimum salary	13,968	14,722	16,637	18,797	19,910	21,187
Midpoint salary	16,430	18,403	20,794	23,582	26,549	30,264
Average increment	410	460	520	598	664	908

Table 4.7: *Relative salary position: the CompaRatio of the minimum salary*

Grade	4	5	6	7	8	9
$\dfrac{\text{Minimum salary}}{\text{Midpoint salary}} * 100$	85	80	80	80	75	70

Note: Refer to percentages in Table 4.2

Table 4.8: *The CompaRatio per employee and for the department as a whole*

Employee	Grade	Actual salary	Midpoint	Compa-Ratio
A	4	14722	16430	90
B	4	16310	16430	99
C	7	21014	23582	89
D	8	25003	26549	94
E	8	22987	26549	87
F	9	29290	30264	97
Total		129326	139804	93

As Tables 4.7 and 4.8 show, the CompaRatio is also a useful tool for analysing the pay policy as it is carried out.

> The CompaRatio offers a comparative measure for the relative
> position of a job or a salary, independent of the grade to which
> the individual employee has been classified

4.11 PERFORMANCE-RELATED PAY INTEGRATED INTO THE SALARY STRUCTURE

If an organisation decided to implement a form of performance-related pay, it must at least meet precondition c if it wants to uphold the essence of such a system. (Precondition c: the performance-

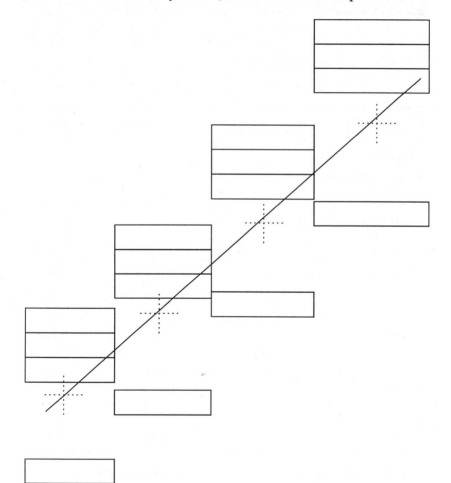

Figure 4.18: *Set-up of integrated performance-related pay*

related pay must be stopped whenever the reasons for granting such allowances cease to exist.) Also preconditions d and e must be taken into account (precondition d: effects of the performance-related pay must be considered; precondition e: the performance-related pay must be linked to the duration and the nature of the performance).

Figure 4.20 demonstrates in which way performance-related pay may be granted.

The distinction between qualitative and quantitative performances and the distinction in reward for each form must be recognisable. For quantitative efforts which are usually of a shorter duration, a direct type of reward is appropriate, for instance in the form of a bonus or more than one increment. The latter is possible when an open scales system is used, but it should be realised that this may cause the system to get 'silted up'. Qualitative performances are usually maintained during a longer period and involve matters such as attitude, inventiveness, initiative etc. For instance, a positive attitude towards the job and the organisation is likely to be of a continuous nature and not incidental. Particularly the continuity of the performance and its determining factors warrants a type of reward that emphasises the prospects rather than the direct income.

To facilitate this the organisation could create not one but, for example, three maximum salaries for each grade. This creates a situation that is similar to the traditional model with several columns for

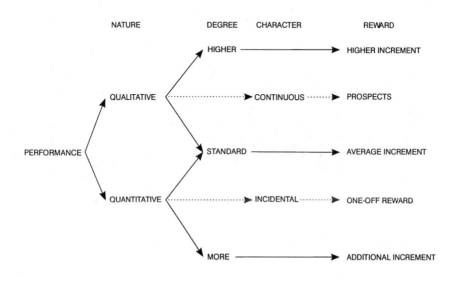

Figure 4.19: *Annual assessment of performance*

each grade (see Table 4.5). These maximum salaries of each grade should have a fixed relation to each other, for instance by having three separate pay policy lines (I, II and III). Each pay policy line has its own maximum salary; the ratios of these maxima to the standard salary may be as follows:

Example I	I = 100 (standard)	II = 106	III = 115
Example II	I = 100 (standard)	II = 107.5	III = 115
Example III	I = 100 (standard)	II = 110	III = 120

Which ratios will be chosen is left to the individual organisation. Depending upon their assessment the salaries of the employees follow pay line I (normal), pay line II (recognisably higher than normal) or III (substantially better than normal) (see Figure 4.21).

When the employee is told to which pay line he has been assigned on the basis of his performance, he must also be informed of the maximum salary that he can reach. This is essential because when it is expected of him that his performances remain at a higher level (future oriented), something should be said on his prospects (also future

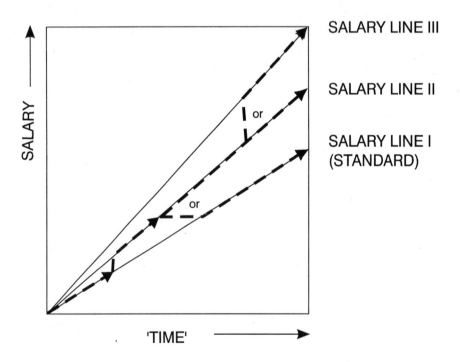

Figure 4.20: *Example of individual salary development*

oriented). If these expectations are no longer met, the consequence is likely to be that the prospects of the employee are reduced in the sense that the expected maximum salary attached to the new pay line to which he has then been assigned is lower. In addition to the differentiation in maximum salary, the size of the average increment can also be adapted. In the case of grade 10 of the example this may have been worked out as follows:

Minimum salary	£24,154	70%
Maximum salary I (standard)	£34,502	100% midpoint
Maximum salary II (standard)	£37,952	110%
Maximum salary III (standard)	£41,402	120%
Average increment I	£1,035	3%
Average increment II	£1,208	3.5%
Average increment III	£1,380	4%

Note: The percentages are based on maximum salary I (standard or midpoint).

If an employee is reassigned to a lower pay line, his actual salary will nominally not be adjusted. If the actual salary should exceed the maximum salary of the lower pay line, the surplus could be granted as an individual allowance or bonus (see also Figure 4.21). The dotted lines show possible courses that the salary of an individual may follow.

As we discussed earlier, there must be an assessment system in place which requires that the reason for the assignment of an individual to one of the pay lines of the grade is well founded and explained to him (precondition f). In addition, the ratios concerning the number of employees – of one or more units of the organisation, not for each grade – that can be assigned to a specific pay line should be established in advance. A major factor for these ratios is the number of pay lines per grade. A limited number of pay lines is preferred because when the number of lines increases, not only will assessing and explaining become more difficult, but it will also be harder to maintain and justify a reasonable distribution of employees over the various pay lines. In practice, three pay lines appear to be sufficient.

When the organisation has opted for three pay lines, it may adopt the following distribution (Figure 4.21):

- at least 75 per cent of the employees should be assigned to pay line I;
- at most 10 per cent of the employees could be assigned to pay line III.

– Different ratios are also feasible, for instance 80 per cent (I) and 5 per cent (III).

The first ratio may have been applied in such a way that, for instance, 75 per cent of the employees are assigned to pay line I, while 25 per cent are assigned to pay line II. In this case nobody is assigned to pay line III. (*Note:* the CompaRatio is always expressed in relation to the maximum of pay line I of the midpoint. A CompaRatio of say 92 is quite possible for all three pay lines (see also Table 4.11).

This type of measure must be developed and implemented in order to manage and control the assessment and evaluation system. If deviations are found, they may induce management to review the way in which people are assessed.

As for any proposal it is recommended that the positive and negative aspects of the system we just have described are summarised and checked against the stated preconditions. Such an evaluation of the model could result in an adjustment to it.

Positive aspects of the model described:

– *Salary adjustment without obstacles caused by the system (precondition a):* Any amount between the minimum and maximum salary of the grade is acceptable.
– *Costs of reassignments (precondition b):* Because the system technically allows any amount to be allotted, there are hardly any implementation costs.
– *Performance versus time (precondition e):* There is a direct link between performance resulting from ambition/attitude and prospects; individual efforts can be reflected in the salary. If an accelerated progress through the grade results in 'pressure' on the maximum for high flyers, opportunities for promotion need to be reviewed (career management).
– *Reversing performance-related pay (precondition c):* Future-oriented performance pay is linked to prospects; a negative assessment results in reducing or terminating prospects for obtaining higher maximum salaries and in a lower average increment or a slower progress to the maximum salary. A negative assessment does not result in a lower salary as such.
– *Benefits (precondition d):* One of the principles of the model is that no salary reduction is required when performances fall back. In this way possible consequences for other benefit entitlements are being avoided.

Negative aspects of the model:

- The method does not provide a conclusive solution for the whole issue of performance-related pay. The method only illustrates how any form of performance-related pay could be incorporated into a remuneration system. The open scales method has the advantage that is no longer necessary to make it possible for employees to trace back any specific salary amount in the grade.
- In any case requirements must be established which the performance-related pay system will have to meet.
- Flexible remuneration systems are bound to fail if the organisation does not have an appropriate personnel information system. This system must be able to establish and demonstrate how the remuneration system is implemented and operated by the organisation.
- Flexible remuneration systems demand a disciplined application. Some organisations think erroneously that all possibilities of the system must be implemented and used as soon as possible. In many cases the result is that the ratios for the distribution of employees over the pay lines are soon be used to their full extent. This implies new employees cannot be reassessed to a higher pay line, and the structure loses its flexibility.
- The amount of salary of an individual cannot be found in the grade. The CompaRatio is difficult to explain to many employees.

Performance-related pay, as it has been discussed in this section, demands above all the courage to communicate bad news to the employee in question. In spite of the fact that if the performance falls back, this will not cause the salary to be *reduced*, this model does not provide a solution to the status problem. Being assigned to a higher pay line involves some advancement in status. This is a problem which organisations should be especially aware of before implementing the above model. If management and the personnel officer in charge ignore this issue, then only half a step is being taken. The organisation should judge whether all effort is warranted and whether such a pay policy really serves its interests.

As in the case of a remuneration system, before starting the development of a performance-related pay system, certain preconditions should be established. The following examples of preconditions of a performance-related pay system may be helpful:

- The superior of the person being assessed has to draw up a written explanation of the assessment.

- The written assessment must be signed by the next higher superior of the person being assessed.
- The assessment must always be given to the person who has been assessed. He must be able to express his comments and any criticism.
- The next higher superior and the personnel officer in charge must always be involved in answering the comments of the employee.
- If the employee being assessed, after having discussed his assessment with his immediate superior, still thinks that he has been judged unfairly, he must be able to invoke the appeal procedure included in the assessment method.

4.12 CAREER REMUNERATION MODEL

In section 4.8 we saw how the traditional salary structure can be changed into more flexible forms of remuneration. This is by no means all that can be said on the possibilities of flexible remuneration. Section 4.8 discussed only the possibilities of the flexible remuneration structure insofar as they concerned pay. Nothing has been said on how a job is assigned to a grade. As indicated in Chapter 1, a development is taking place in this field that has resulted in the job level matrix. This is a matrix with job families on the vertical axis and grades on the horizontal axis (see Table 2.6). If we combine the possibilities of the job level matrix with those of a flexible remuneration structure, we have an instrument with which the salaries of employees throughout their career can be managed relatively simply.

This career remuneration model makes it relatively easy to assign employees to grades and determine an appropriate salary. It also offers the possibility of rewarding both qualitative and quantitative achievements. The main precondition is discipline. As with the broadening of other rules and opportunities, the career remuneration model requires discipline in its application. We will illustrate this by means of the sample job of Secretary.

The job of Secretary can be assigned to grade 5 of the job family secretariat (see Table 4.10) which is part of the total job family matrix (JFM). As can be seen from this table, similar jobs exist at different levels, in this example in grades 4, 5, 6 and 7. Therefore it is not necessary to make a separate job description for each level. In consultation with the employee and his immediate superior it can be established what the requirements of the job are and to which grade the job should be assigned. No separate job description is required, no grad-

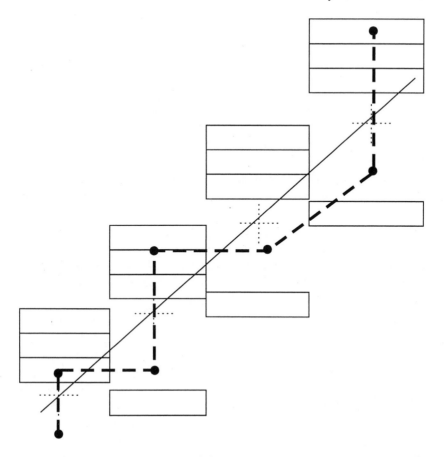

Figure 4.21: *Set-up of the career remuneration model*

ing, no meeting of the evaluation committee and no (external) expert. In this case the Personnel Department or a specialist from the head office is able to monitor the whole process, to keep the JFM up to date as the system-holder and to act as adviser.

If in time a job has become heavier or when a permanent position has become vacant, it must be determined to what extent an employee from a lower grade meets the job requirements which have been laid down in the JFM. Next, the job-holder can be assigned to a grade. It is obvious that the employee is classified to a higher job grade exclusively on the basis of his personal qualifications, although in practice this problem occurs quite frequently. Of course, an organisation wants to offer each employee a job that suits his qualifications and competences best, but it must also avoid incurring wage costs that are not strictly necessary. In addition, other employees will perceive this as preferential treatment and start to doubt the objectivity of the assignment procedure. In the JFM a career can progress horizontally as well as vertically.

The next step concerns determining the remuneration in accordance with the grade to which the job has been assigned. (See also section 4.8.) Figure 4.24 illustrates how an employee, on the basis of his individual performances, progresses from the minimum salary to the maximum in the grade. The example is randomly chosen. Placing a job on a higher or lower pay line does not need to follow the obvious order of I > II > III or the other way round. It is also possible to assign a job from pay line I to III. If an employee who, within his grade, was assigned to pay line II or III is reassigned to a higher or lower grade, he should be placed at pay line I of that new grade.

If an employee is assigned to a new grade, a new assessment of his performance should be made on the basis of the new (and usually higher) job requirements. Therefore placing the employee on pay line I is a logical step. Both employee and organisation are not able to give guarantees concerning the new performance level of the employee. Performing and assessing the performance against the job requirements is a continuous process. The reward of the performance fluctuates in accordance with the results of this assessment.

In designing the salary structure this facility should be kept in mind. It may create problems if the progression in the salary structure is lower than the difference between the maximum salaries of successive pay lines. This is illustrated in Table 4.9.

| Grade | | | Maximum salaries | |
	Grade Line I 100%		Grade Line II 110%	Grade Line III 120%
4	16430	(100%)	18073	19760
5	18403	(+12%)	20243	22084
6	20794	(+13%)	22873	24953
7	23582	(+13%)	25940	28298

Table 4.9: *Differences between maximum salaries of pay lines and the progression within the grade*

The percentage (12 and 13 per cent) after the amounts of £18,403 and £20,794 represents the difference (progression) in relation to the amount of £16,430.

It will be clear that an employee who has been classified to pay line III of grade 5 and has reached the maximum salary of £22,084 will not be satisfied with a reassignment to grade 6, line I, because the maximum salary there is lower than he has already reached in grade 5.

As Table 4.10 shows, the job family secretariat has four consecutive job levels. All these jobs have been assigned to either grade 4, 5, 6 and 7 which allows a salary to grow from £13,968 (minimum salary of grade 4) to £28,298 (maximum salary of grade 7, pay line III). If in this example the amount of £13,968 is set at 100 per cent, then the prospect in this series of an amount of £28,298 equals 195 per cent; almost double the original amount.

Table 4.10: *Level indicators and sample summaries on which Figures 4.22 and 4.23 are based*

Job family secretariat

Grade	4	5	6	7
Level	Technical operational activities according to guidelines with indicator direct supervision. Possibly operationally in charge of some employees carrying out routine activities	Technical work with co-ordinating, preparatory and operational elements. Possibly operationally in charge of some technical employees who carry out operational activities	Specialist operational activities according to guidelines with a large degree of autonomy. Possibly operationally in charge of some technical employees	Specialist activities with co-ordinating, preparatory and mainly operational elements. Usually operationally in charge of some technical employees
Sample	Performing typing work (from drafts) and routine secretarial summary tasks of a simple nature. Performing some limited administrative tasks related to this typing work, such as: making appointments, filing, copying of documents.	Performing various secretarial tasks of a routine nature, such as typing from draft (some in a foreign language), drafting routine letters, taking down shorthand notes. Taking minutes of meetings. Carrying out routine administrative tasks, such as: typing, making appointments and itineraries, handling mail, starting and maintaining files	Performing full secretarial standard tasks such as: carrying out various repetitive activities without assistance and within clear terms of reference, initiating the follow-up of actions by superior, taking down shorthand notes, drafting routine letters, handling the mail without consulting others. Carrying out standard administrative tasks, such as typing, collecting and summarising data according to instructions, designing/managing the files, possibly directing typists and other secretaries	Performing full secretarial tasks of relatively high responsibility and of a confidential nature, such as: carrying out various repetitive activities without assistance and within general terms of reference. Interpreting issues and taking action, setting up subsystems for specific tasks, taking down shorthand notes, taking minutes, drafting letters (possibly in a foreign language). Organising meetings and business trips Possibly managing typists and other secretaries

If we combine the possibilities of the JFM with those of the flexible remuneration structure, we arrive at a model that can best be called the career remuneration model (CRM). When hiring an employee or assigning or re-evaluating a job it will be checked whether this person or job meets the criteria which have been laid down for each grade in the JFM. Next, this assessment is translated into the assignment of the employee or job to one of the four grades. Depending upon the level of the employee and the job requirements at the start of the employment, the job can be entered at any level between the minimum salary of grade 4 and the maximum salary of grade 7. The only (systems) requirement of the starting salary agreed is that the amount must lie within the salary range of the chosen grade. After that there will be no need to complete a new job description and evaluation at each change during the rest of his career. A check as to whether the requirements of the method are met is sufficient when agreeing the next step in his career with the employer.

With this method not only vertical career steps can be managed. It can also be used to explain where and why a further (vertical) progress is no longer possible. Next, depending upon the availability of suitable permanent positions, the possibilities of a horizontal career development can be investigated.

To summarise, it can be said that depending upon the availability of positions the progress of the individual employee through this career remuneration model is governed by:

- the job level (level indicators and sample summaries)
- assessment of the functioning of the employee (pay line)
- assessment of the quantitative performance (granting one or more increments)

Of course the CRM has the same positive and negative aspects as the flexible salary structure as described in section 4.11.

The CRM offers great flexibility for the development of employees, while on the other hand a number of assessments have been built in that puts a break on the progress in the case of a negative assessment.

Next, we describe the procedure for adjusting the salary within the open scales structure with several pay lines, within the context of the CRM as elaborated in Table 4.11 and illustrated in Figures 4.27 and 4.28.

Table 4.11: *Progress of an employee through various grades*

Action	Grade 4	Grade 5	Grade 6	Grade 7	Compa-Ratio
Hiring: Assignment to pay line 1	13,968				85
Increment	14,378				88
Assignment of functioning: assign to pay line II	14,793				90
Increment	15,243				93
Testing against job requirements: assign to grade 5		15,703			85
Assessment of functioning: assign to pay line II		16,213			88
Testing against job requirements: assign to grade 6			16,733		80
Increment			17,253		83
Assessment of functioning: assign to pay line II			17,833		86
Increment			18,413		89
Assessment of performance grant 2 increments			19,573		94
Increment			20,153		97
Testing against job requirements: assign to grade 7				20,751	88
Assessment of performance: grant 2 increments				21,947	92
Increment				22,545	96
Assessment of functioning: assign to pay line III				23,355	96
Increment				24,165	102
Increment				24,975	106

Figure 4.23 shows how an employee can progress through the various grades. Here are some considerations on the course of this 'growth line' in Figures 4.23 and 4.24:

– The difference between two consecutive grades is relatively small, as is evident from the level indicators and the sample summaries in Table 4.10. This implies that the step to a higher grade is relatively easily made.
– If an employee is classified in a higher grade, he is usually placed at pay line I.
– If the difference between two consecutive grades is relatively small, the step to the next higher grade can be seen as a re-evaluation. If the career steps are larger, for instance when an employee is reassigned from grade 5 to grade 7, there is a rather marked difference in the weight of the requirements of the job. In that case such steps could be called a promotion.
– It is more obvious to offer an employee on pay line III a promotion instead of a re-evaluation. In practice a re-evaluation is more likely when the employee is on pay line I or II. (See also section 4.11 for the requirement for placement on one of the pay lines.)

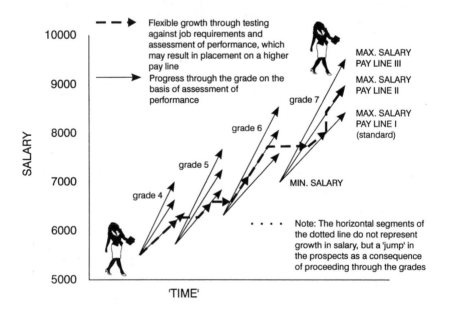

Figure 4.22: *The career remuneration model: steps through the various grades*

In Figure 4.24 a promotion is visualised from grade percentage, pay line III to grade 7, pay line I. It shows that the employee is ready for a new challenge, because the difference in level between grades 5 and 7 is substantial. An employee assigned to pay line III can be expected to be able to perform well on that higher level of grade 7. Figure 4.23 illustrates just what happens in the case of a re-evaluation of the job or a reassessment of the job-holder.

Using the CRM offers more opportunities to differentiate the remuneration than the traditional salary structure. The need for such differentiation depends on the developments in the labour market for specific job families (see Table 5.4). A (temporary) higher valuation on the market as, for example, jobs in the field of automation, may cause an increase in the total remuneration level of this 'column' in the JFM relative to the other job families. If this increase is no longer expedient, because in the market the salaries for this job family have decreased to a level that is comparable with that of other job families, the old situation can be restored. This may be achieved by temporarily suspending structural increases of the salaries in the grade concerned.

In fact this adds a new dimension to the salary structure, which now in total consists of the following elements:

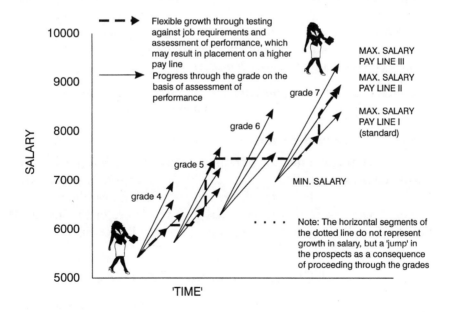

Figure 4.23: *The career remuneration model: re-evaluation and promotion within the same job family*

- salary grades of bands;
- job levels which are based on standards laid down in the JFM (referring to the ideal situation);
- additional increments on the basis of the performance;
- differences in pay levels of various job families depending upon the situation in the labour market.

Advantages of the Career Remuneration Model

- the model can easily absorb changing conditions in the labour market (see section 4.8 on preconditions);
- the model makes it clear to the employees what prospects and possibilities for development exist in the organisation and how growth and development will be remunerated in the technical sense;
- the model provides clear, crucial decision points (see Figures 4.23 and 4.24) which make it possible to manage the development and the career of individual employees more precisely.
- the model offers insight into opportunities for both vertical and horizontal development as well as into the prospects which the various job families offer.
- the model does not enforce predetermined reassignments to grades. As every job is part of a job family, a job-holder may start in a lower grade than the ultimately intended grade. If, after a predetermined assessment period the employee performs satisfactorily, he can be classified in the intended grade.

The model offers the opportunity to differentiate the pay policy in accordance with developments in the labour market.

Disadvantages of the CRM

As with any flexible method of remunerating or classifying jobs, the CRM requires discipline on the side of the assessor. Not only are individual capabilities of employees important, but also the number of permanent positions and their design (we also refer to what has been said in the Introduction under the heading 'Rationale').

4.13 CHECKLIST REMUNERATION

A checklist for the remuneration issue should be quite extensive in order to treat all possible considerations as a basis for the development of a balanced pay policy. In addition to primary terms of employment (remuneration), the checklist also deals with secondary (benefits) and tertiary terms, because these constitute an integral part of the remuneration issue.

Basic principles of a remuneration policy

— What are the mutual relationships between the primary, secondary and other components of the remuneration policy? Which element is considered to be the most important?
— What constitutes the basis of the salary structure?
— Does the organisation want to have an autonomous remuneration policy or a policy which is derived from collective labour agreements?
— Does the organisation want to pursue a rigid or a more flexible remuneration policy? How disciplined is management in applying the systems?
— Is the organisation considering implementing one or possibly more new job evaluations? How familiar and comfortable is the organisation with the phenomenon of job evaluation? What are the reasons for selecting one or several specific methods?
— Is the organisation considering implementing a performance assessment system? In what way, if at all, do the results of this assessment influence the remuneration level of individual employees or groups of employees?
— What should be the relationship between the remuneration level of higher and lower jobs? What are the effects on the gross/net pay ratio?
— Are exceptions allowed in the remuneration of specific jobs or job families in comparison with others in order to follow developments in the labour market?

On what criteria does the organisation want to base the differences in pay?

— Differences in the weight of jobs?
— Does it want to promote growth in the jobs or rather promotions?
— Differences in experience and seniority?
— Does it want, or will it allow, differences in pay for one and the same job? Does it want such differences on all levels of jobs?

How should the remuneration system be communicated?

- Has every employee access to information on the salary structure/regulations?
- Is it useful/desirable to formulate strict rules to ensure the correct application of the system? Should every employee be able to verify the correct application?

Construction of the system

- Does the salary system function well?
- What are the financial consequences of a reassignment to another (higher/lower) grade. What is regarded as a re-evaluation of a job; what is a promotion? Should each of these result in differences in remuneration?
- Does the organisation intend to implement a form of performance-related pay and how will these rewards be linked to the salary scale? How large should the difference be between marginal performances and 'excellent' performances? How many 'levels' of performance are there and have these levels been clearly defined? Is there a standard against which performance is measured?
- What are the rules for applying variable remuneration?
- What solution will be chosen for employees whose salaries do not fit into the grade to which they should be classified?
- Have these rules for the application of the pay policy been laid down in a document on the rules and regulations on remuneration?
- Which forms of appeal against the results of a job evaluation and personnel assessment are open to the employee?

Parameters of the salary system

- Should a difference in the weight of jobs, however small, always result in a difference in salary, or should the salaries of those jobs remain the same for a certain period of time (overlap in grades)? How large is that overlap allowed to be?
- How large is the difference in remuneration between the highest and lowest job? Is this spread perceived to be fair? How many grades should there be between these highest and lowest salaries? Is the line between these highest and lowest salaries uninterrupted or should there be 'breaks'?
- How large is the difference between the minimum and maximum salary of a grade and is this difference the same in all grades ?

- What progression should there be between grades, ie should the difference be as a percentage between consecutive (maximum salaries of) grades? Where more than one job evaluation method is used, how far does that correspond with differences in weight of jobs according to the standards in these job evaluation methods?
- Is there a link between the minimum and maximum salaries in the various grades and the ages of employees? For instance, is the minimum salary for all grades set for the same age?
- In what way does the salary progress within a grade, eg through steps or through a system of flexible increments?
- If a system of performance-related pay is used, how large is the variable part of the salary allowed to be at the most in relation to the total (fixed) salary?
- To what extent does the variable part of the remuneration count with respect to other terms of employment, for instance the pension basis? Is it possible to prevent this?

5

Salary surveys

5.1 INTRODUCTION

Income or salary surveys (remuneration comparisons) are carried out by several (commercial) agencies, groups of companies and associations. They cover most elements of the terms of employment of the participants, including salaries and other conditions and benefits. The reason for this is that only all these terms in their mutual relationships can constitute a sound basis for testing and comparing the remuneration policy of an individual company. Some agencies calculate the value of the benefits and other benefits in order to arrive at a total income or total remuneration of the job surveyed. Most agencies and firms indicate only to what extent certain benefits are used. In this way they offer a starting point to companies that want to establish whether their policy differs from other participants of the survey. Participating in a salary survey also provides insight into the relationship between salary (direct pay) on the one hand and benefits on the other hand. In this chapter we will concentrate on comparing the salary conditions, ie the remuneration, and discuss the content of a salary survey, possible set-ups and how far the results of the surveys of different agencies are comparable.

An organisation may decide to participate in a salary survey for various reasons. The most obvious is to be able to compare its own salary level with that of other organisations. Also the relationships between salaries within the organisation compared with those of others may be useful, because in this way differences in the remuneration for specific jobs and job families will become apparent.

Salary surveys can be divided into two large groups:

- surveys based on job evaluation points;
- surveys based on job titles and a short summary of the job content.

The first type of salary survey compares jobs on the basis of their (relative) weight. These comparisons usually involve only the job evaluation points and salaries. In the second type of survey a series of job titles is accompanied by a short summary of activities and responsibilities and of the context and the place of the job within the organisation. Through a matching process the relative 'weight' of jobs is established. In contrast to surveys on the basis of job evaluation points, the comparisons are made against various criteria, such as age, seniority, sales, number of employees which report to the job, etc.

Salary surveys use statistical calculation models which may be quite complicated, partly depending upon the type of survey. In most cases the Personnel Officer is at the mercy of the organiser of the survey where it concerns the interpretation and reliability of the results of the survey. This is an aspect which certainly deserves more attention by the agencies and which is the reason why associations and groups of companies have started their own 'club surveys'. These club surveys have the advantage that they can focus on aspects and issues that are of particular interest to the members/participants. The demand for surveys of specific jobs and job families may also have played a role. It is thus not surprising that the larger agencies and consultancy firms also try to meet these needs.

In this chapter we will discuss the salary surveys of the following firms:

- Hay Management Consultants;
- Towers Perrin;
- Watson Wyatt.

In order to provide a maximum insight into the meaning of the outcome of these surveys, they are simulated. Therefore we have asked each firm to clearly indicate in what way they process the data and how the calculations are made. For the comparison between these surveys we have a database of approximately 2,250 job-holders in some 15 companies. The necessary calculations were made using the statistical software package SPSS PC+. Thanks to the help of the support department of this software company, we have been able to obtain a sound insight into the differences between the three salary surveys.

Table 5.1 lists the elements that are taken into consideration in our investigation.

Table 5.1:   *Set-up of the model for comparing salary surveys*

	Elements
Job	JEP Survey based on job evaluation points – Results of job evaluation as a total number of points
	JTS Survey based on job summary – Job title with short summary of content – Reporting level – Number of employees job-holder is in charge of – Required level of education
Job-holder	- Age – Number of years in employment – Number of years in job
Environment (factors within the company)	– Sales of company – Total number of employees of organisation – Type of organisation; domestic or foreign parent company

In surveys on the basis of job title plus summary (JTS), the organising agency usually provides a diagram showing the relationship between the various types of jobs, as well as their organisational context. This does not prevent serious errors from being made sometimes, in particular in the case of corporations with a division structure, organisation split-ups in groups of operating companies and business units.

With regard to surveys on the basis of job evaluation points (JEP), it must be kept in mind that various job families and lines of business are sometimes grouped together too easily, arguing that similar point scores would make these comparable. Definitions of concepts used are essential to ensure a correct input and interpretation of the outcomes. Unfortunately, the contents of these definitions may vary considerably between system-holders. Some organisations make a distinction between a fixed and a variable component of share profits. An example of this is that, whenever a company makes a profit, a fixed percentage of the salary will be paid. The size of the variable components depends then in part upon the actual size of the profit. If such a system is used, the fixed and the variable parts of the profit-sharing need to be proportionally allocated to the basic salary and the total cash.

Without exception all firms use the following statistical level indicators for the labour market.

D9: Ninth or upper decile

The ninth decile represents the level at which 10 per cent of the observations have a score or value higher than that level and the remaining 90 per cent a lower one.

Q3: Third or upper quartile

The third quartile represents the level at which 25 per cent of the observations have a score or a value higher than that level and the remaining 75 per cent a lower one.

M: Median

The median represents the middle observation.

A: Average or mean

The average is the arithmetical middle of the value or scores of the observations.

Q1: First or lower quartile

The first quartile represents the level at which 75 per cent of the observations have a score or value higher than that level and the remaining 25 per cent have a lower one.

D1: First or lower decile

The first decile represents the level at which 90 per cent of the observations have a score or value higher than that level and the remaining 10 per cent have a lower one.

There may be some differences in the names that are used for these concepts in the sense that the first decile/quartile is called the lowest and the lowest decile/quartile the first.

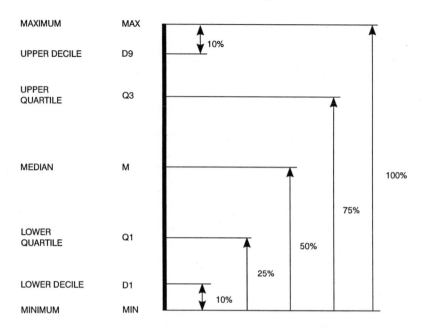

Figure 5.1: *Meaning of the concepts decile and quartile*

5.2 CONDITIONS AND REQUIREMENTS

Each agency that carries out a salary survey sets its conditions for participation. However, none stipulates the requirements which the investigation should meet. Nevertheless these requirements are decisive for the quality of the survey and the credibility of its results. We therefore give some examples of requirements of both the participating organisations and the jobs included in the survey.

Preconditions that should be met as far as possible by the *participating organisations*

1. Participating organisations are preferably from the same industry or line of business. The size of the business and of the participating organisation are also important factors. Jobs in automation are differently valued/rewarded in software firms from those, for example, in paper companies. The distinction between companies and non-profit organisations is important.
2. If the survey also wants to investigate the salaries of jobs lower in the hierarchy, this should be done on a regional level, rather than on a national level. Employees for these jobs are usually recruited regionally and not nationally.

3. Companies in the survey, which in general pay relatively high salaries, are less important to the companies with a relatively low level of remuneration.
4. The composition of the total pay package, and the policy concerning the relationships between pay, benefits and other provisions, influence the results of the survey to such an extent that wrong conclusions may be drawn.
5. Participating organisations should co-operate where possible and ensure the highest possible level of consistency of the input. Large changes in the survey population have a noticeable influence on the results of the investigation.

Preconditions which the *jobs/job-holders* must meet

1. The job must be representative for the job family to which it belongs. For each job family jobs of various levels must be included.
2. The jobs must be comparable externally. It makes little sense to include jobs which are specific to a particular company, because these are not comparable with others or are only comparable by chance.
3. The jobs should be relatively stable. Functions of which the content frequently changes or jobs with a high turnover rate are bad material for comparison. The remuneration level for these jobs depends too much on coincidence.
4. The jobs must have been described clearly and preferably concisely (in the case of a job title survey). If not, comparisons become difficult.
5. If carried out consistently and in a controlled fashion, job evaluation provides a very useful contribution to the comparisons.

Preconditions which must be met by the *consultancy firms* carrying out a salary survey.

1. In the case of a survey on the basis of job evaluation points, the consistency with which the job evaluation is used must be carefully monitored. Job inflation could result in shifts in the remuneration practice, as will be demonstrated in this report.
2. In the case of a survey on the basis of job titles plus summaries, care must be taken that the job summaries are correctly interpreted when applied to the jobs of the participant. Job summaries must be of high quality, to make real comparisons possible. Personal guidance from the consultant of the organising firm is required. In addition, the place of the job in the organisation must be clearly delineated.
3. Set-up and format of the report sent to the participants must allow for comparisons across several years. New elements added to the survey must be clearly pointed out.
4. For data collection the consultancy firms in general use questionnaires. Practice shows that these questionnaires quite frequently change in format. This not only causes differences in interpretation, but requires extra effort from the participating organisations. Restraint is in a sense a precondition.
5. The report should in clear terms provide insight into the statistical calculation methods that have been used. The interested participant should be able to compare (other) jobs in his company (again) with the information from the survey.
6. Graphs should be easily readable. The use of logarithmic scales should be restricted to what is absolutely necessary. A graph is only useful if the values at the X- and Y-axes are clearly indicated and can be read accurately. It is not so important if this requirement results in straight or curved lines.

The degree to which the various elements of the requirements are fulfilled has a major impact on the results of the investigation and the salary surveys.

As we pointed out earlier, a salary survey can be set up and implemented in a number of ways:

– as a survey on the basis of job evaluation points (JEP), or on the basis of job titles plus summaries (JTS);

- adding elements which the investigator thinks important for reasons of comparison;
- addressed to different participating organisations and jobs.

In carrying out the salary surveys, agencies and consulting firms may use the following calculation methods:

Determining quartiles

For each job (in a survey on the basis of job titles plus summaries) or each measuring point (in surveys on the basis of job evaluation points) the values of the upper and lower quartiles and the median of the values (salaries) obtained are calculated. Thus for the same job, or for the same job level, all quartile values are calculated.

Linear or multiple regression analysis

Regression analyses are used to determine and test the relationships between a number of elements (independent variable) and the salary (dependent variable). An example is provided by the Hay method which opted here for an approach on the basis of linear regression calculus to determine the relation between job evaluation score and salary for each individual participant. The Tower Perrin method has opted for the non-linear multiple regression approach.

Regression calculations combined with determination of quartile values

For each participating organisation the (linear or multiple) regression line is determined. For each measuring point in the job evaluation surveys, quartile values of all regression lines are calculated. The Hay survey may also serve here as an example for the presentation of the survey results to all participants; in the report it includes the line of central tendency.

5.3 SALARY SURVEYS

5.3.1 Hay Management Consultants

In their survey report Hay Management Consultants clearly distinguish between their salary survey and the so-called 'packages comparisons'. In the latter, emphasis is on benefits and tertiary provisions for employees. The Hay Remuneration Survey is typically tailored to participants who use the Hay method for job evaluation and job profiling.

In a number of 'job families surveys' a different approach is taken. There the basis of the comparisons is the total score of the job (in a job evaluation based survey) as determined through the Hay method. The job evaluation process within the participating organisations is tested by Hay against its standard evaluations. Deviations from this standard are rectified and adjusted before the potential participant is admitted to the survey.

Table 5.2: *Comparative model of the salary survey by Hay Management Consultants based on job evaluation*

JEP Survey	
Job	– Total score covering factors such as job content, required level of education and number of employees reporting to the job
Job-holder	– Not applicable
Context	– Total score covering factors such as sales, budget size, type of organisation

The core of Hay's salary survey consists of a number of graphs which reflect the situation on the market (Figure 5.2). The graphs are made for basic salary and total pay, and differentiate between participants with a variable remuneration system and those without such a system.

The essence of the method used is as follows. For each participant the regression line is calculated, assessed and, if necessary, adjusted on the basis of a total review of the participant's data. Hay applies strict rules for this calculation method and the assessment of the outcome (regression line), paying special attention to the effects caused by the input of new participants in the survey.

A large number of companies participate in this salary survey which covers tens of thousands of jobs. The huge amount of regression lines produced by this number of participants would make the graphs unreadable and incomprehensible, because lines of individual participants would barely be distinguishable. This is why Hay calculates the percentiles (upper decile, upper quartile, median, lower quartile and lower decile) for a series of fixed measuring points. Next, a graph is constructed for each participant which compares the pay policy line of that participant with these percentiles.

Hay differentiates between participants with variable remuneration systems and those without, because this results in practice in clear differences in the basic salaries. Each graph is accompanied by a table providing the formulas for both quartiles and the median with which sample points on the regression line can be calculated. The formulas (see Table 5.3) are provided only for segments of the lines in the graphs (see Figure 5.2), because the percentile lines are not straight.

In order to make comparisons with the results of salary surveys of other firms, we have drawn a separate graph for the job of Profit Centre Manager in which the pay practice is shown both on the basis of the points scored according to the Hay method, and on the basis of sales.

Table 5.3: *Formulae for calculating individual positions on the pay policy line from Figure 5.2*

Market line	Hay points	Formula*
Q3	100–300	46.8P + 7654
	300–800	53.78P + 5559
M	100–400	48.49P + 6798
	400–800	45.31P + 8071
	800–900	87.26P – 25491
	900–1000	32.98P + 23361
Q1	100–400	44.41P + 5428
	400–500	64.93P – 2778
	500–600	22.25P + 18562
	600–700	71.37P – 10910

*For P the number of Hay points must be substituted.

Details included in the report are:

- comparisons of wage costs and net pay for a number of European countries;
- list of participating organisations;
- summary of the characteristics of groups of participants;
- comparison of pay practice and pay policy;
- difference in remuneration between large, medium-sized and small companies;
- comparisons of total cash for various functional areas (see Table 5.4).

Table 5.4 *Comparison of differences in remuneration of functional areas or job families*

Functional area	<300	300–600	600–1000	>1000
All jobs	100 (38)	100 (41)	100 (46)	100 (48)
General management	–	–	–	106 (48)
Finance/accounting/				
controlling	101 (37)	100 (39)	99 (43)	103 (47)
Automation				
Personnel	97 (39)	98 (41)	99 (45)	101 (47)
Sales				
etc				

Note: The average ages of job-holders are given between brackets. The numbers give the ratio to the totals of all participants in the category.

Also details are provided on:

– the impact of differences of age;
– trends in the labour market concerning basic pay and total cash in the previous five years;
– developments in the growth of individual salaries (separate chapter);
– the expected growth of salaries in the coming period running from 2 July to 1 July of the following year.

5.3.2 Towers Perrin

Towers Perrin produces and sells a report that concentrates on comparing salary policy and salary practice. In addition, it includes comparisons of a series of benefits and tertiary provisions for employees. The report also contains a rather (too) concise explanation on the statistical analysis methods used by this firm. As a basis for these comparisons Towers Perrin uses the job title plus a short summary of the content of the job. The participant and Towers Perrin's consultant jointly establish whether the function in question is lighter, equal or heavier than the standard job of Towers Perrin.

In its survey based on job title plus summary, Towers Perrin follows a somewhat different approach in that it relates the position of

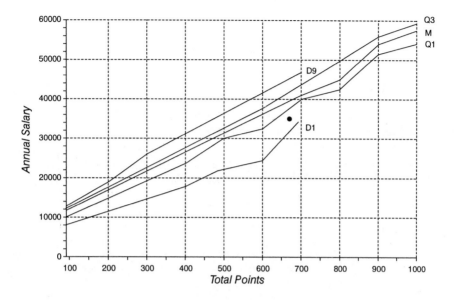

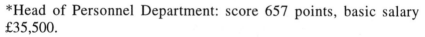

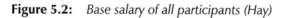

*Head of Personnel Department: score 657 points, basic salary £35,500.

Figure 5.2: *Base salary of all participants (Hay)*

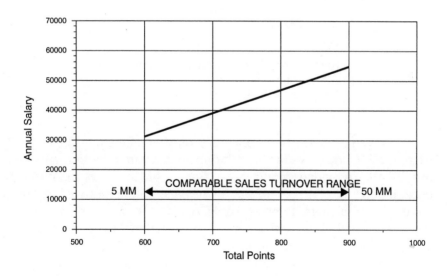

Figure 5.3: *Basic salary of Profit Centre Manager related to sales (Hay)*

each individual job-holder to the labour market conditions (see Table 5.5). Using multiple regression analysis the survey investigates at the same time the impact of various individual remuneration factors and combinations of factors. Specifically multiple regression analysis is applied to factors that:

– determine the remuneration of individual job-holders;
– influence the predicted remuneration.

Table 5.5: *Comparative model of the salary survey by Towers Perrin – the standard job of Towers Perrin*

JT Survey	
Job	– Job title plus short summary of the content of the job Comparisons with 'own' job are made at three levels – Level of education required by job – Level to which the job reports – Member of the Board – Number of employees reporting to the job – International experience – Eligible (or not) for bonus
Job-holder	– Age – Number of years in employment – Number of years in job
Context	– Sales – Total number of employees of the organisation – Industry/line of business – Type of organisation, eg local subsidiary, regional

A total summary in the form of a graph illustrating the position of the participating organisation in relation to the other participants is usually only provided upon request. Such a graph shows the difference in value of: 1 of pay of the 'own' organisation and 1 of pay of the other participants. In other words, the X-axis of the graph shows the salary level of the participating organisation, while the Y-axis shows the corresponding salary level of the other participants. There is still another difference, compared with other salary surveys. The data of the 'own' organisation is separated from the data of other participants. In this way the position of the participating organisation can be clearly contrasted with that of the other participants, without affecting the position of those participants.

The first comparison in the survey report between basic salary and total cash is based on calculations of Q1, M and Q3 of the actual amounts. The tables are made 'for all participants' with a separate one for the individual participant. The latter shows the position of each of the jobs covered by the survey.

Next, a table (5.6) is given in which each individual job of the participating organisation is compared with the market rate. Multiple regression analyses are used to compare the position of the job-holder with the market rates and of the job itself and the market rates.

Table 5.6: *Position comparison table*

Towers Perrin Remuneration Database Position Summary Table All Participants Analyses – Revenue Group 2 £51 – £200 Million						
Position title: Profit Centre Manager Job code: 101 Total cases: 71						
Pay data	*Your data*	*Valid cases*	*25% ILE*	*Mean*	*Median*	*75% ILE*
Base pay (£)	48398	71	31607	37630	35376	42874
Actual bonus(£)	11715	59	5125	7510	6131	10644
Other cash (£)	1343	59	N/A	671	671	1343
Total cash (£)	61457	71	55440	62348	64199	74297
Car value (£)	16790	59	16790	16790	16790	15670
Last base % increase	3	55	4	6	5	9
Month since adjustment	2	65	1	3	3	3
Target bonus *	25	61	N/A	18	17	36
Maximum bonus*	25	61	N/A	N/A	N/A	N/A
Annual bonus EI		55	are eligible			
Share options EI		4	are eligible			
Other LTI EI		1	are eligible			

[*I]% of base

Scope data

| Sales (£M) | 115 | 71 | 51 | 81 | 88 | 125 |
| Employees | 210 | 71 | 92 | 125 | 134 | 251 |

Incumbent data

Age	48	71	37	43	43	47
Years in service	19	55	5	10	8	14
Years in position	6	59	1	4	4	6
EES supervised	12	59	2	7	4	8

Job impact data

Board membership	1 Subsid Exec	0 Subsid Co	0 Corp Exec	0 Main B
Reporting level – this entity	0 RL 1	1 RL 2	6 RL 3	5 RL 4
Reporting level – total organisation	0 RL 1	0 RL 2	0 RL 3	0 RL 4
International responsibility	45 None	12 Incident	0 Signific	0 Major
Job match	0 are +	18 are –		

The remainder of the survey report provides:

- information on the use of variable remuneration systems as part of the remuneration policy and as a practical solution;
- the proportion of their total salary which the job-holders receive as bonus, as well as the average amounts and percentages of the bonus (provided in a separate table for each job title);
- information on the development of consumer prices;
- budgets for pay rises/reviews;
- overview of company cars given to holders of each job as well as the average value of company cars;
- information on expense accounts;
- information on sundry provisions and facilities;
- overview of job titles and summaries.

Finally we give some examples of job summaries that Towers Perrin uses in its survey.

ERD – Capsule job descriptions

Job code	**21 Quality Assurance Manager**
Alternative position title	**Quality Control Manager**
Job purpose	To maintain and improve quality of manufacturing processes and finished goods to meet customer/internal requirements
Typical responsibilities	Develops, defines and audits quality standards, measures and methods throughout the design, procurement and manufacturing processes; establishes and maintains inspection and control procedures; increases quality awareness in the manufacturing function, eg through training, quality initiatives; may have responsibility for total quality management programme
Reporting structure	Typically reports to Head of Manufacturing or to Plant Manager; manages a small team of QA technicians; reporting level 3/4
Typical minimum experience/knowledge	Technical degree: eight years' relevant experience

Job code	**22 Engineering Manager**
Alternative position title	**Manufacturing Engineering Manager**
Job purpose	To provide technical/engineering support for the production processes
Typical responsibilities	Advises on production methods, quality and procedures, changes and installation of equipment; defines production processes and techniques, including writing technical company documents; liaises with external suppliers and consulting firms as appropriate; may be responsible for plant maintenance
Reporting structure	Typically reports to Head of Manufacturing or Plant Manager; manages a team of engineers; reporting level 3/4.
Typical minimum experience/knowledge	Degree, qualified engineer; eight years' relevant experience

5.3.3 Watson Wyatt

A distinctive feature of the Watson Wyatt report is the extensive information it contains on the statistical techniques used. This information is useful for understanding the formulas with which the individual salary of, for instance, a senior executive can be calculated or determined. However, it is somewhat confusing that in the explanation of the calculation methods and the sample calculations attached, in some cases the influence of age and number of years in the job are demonstrated, whereas in others immediately following, they are not. No explanation is given. In addition, age and seniority are not taken into account in the formulas represented in the graphs (Figure 5.4). In calculating the amount of salary these formulas include only the factors of sales and hierarchical level.

All jobs included in the report are represented in tabular form. The amounts in the tables are the quartile and decile amounts directly calculated on the basis of the factual salary amounts. The individual salary amounts in the 'own' organisation are not represented in the tables. In order to be able to determine the correct position of the organisation itself relative to the general data in the Watson Wyatt salary survey report, the organisation has to preserve its own input data carefully.

The format of the report is the same for all countries in which Watson Wyatt publishes salary surveys.

The report provides information on direct pay and benefits. Its basis consists of short summaries of job which, in addition to a brief description of the content, give a clear indication of the position of the job within the organisational context. For this the report uses a model of an organisation chart which comprises all the jobs in the organisation included in the survey. The content of the job will be classified into three levels: A, B and C. The individual jobs of the own organisation are matched to these levels in order to establish their specific levels. In the calculations and comparisons concerning jobs of senior executives, factors such as level of sales, age, number of years in the job, are taken into account. The factual pay practice of the organisation is determined through multiple regression analyses.

JT Survey	
Job	Job title with short summary at three levels: A, B and C
Job-holder	Age
	Number of years in job
Context	Sales

The core of the report is the tables containing information for each job. This information provides insight into the following characteristics (see Table 5.7):

- *characteristics of the total sample*, including details on sales, manpower, age and years in the job;
- *direct pay*, giving details on the pay practice for the three levels as a whole (A + B + C) and for each of the individual levels;
- *bonuses and sales commission*, the number of persons receiving a bonus as well as the level of bonuses as a percentage of the salary. Similar information is provided on sales commission.

The basic salary (which Watson Wyatt calls *annual base salary* or *ABS*) corresponds with the definitions given in this chapter. The same is true for total cash (which Watson Wyatt calls *annual total remuneration* or *ATR*).

This report, too, starts with information on the participating organisations, a review of trends and developments in salaries in the previous period and a preview of the expected increases in pay for the coming period. Company cars are discussed and details are given on company use of private cars and sundry benefits.

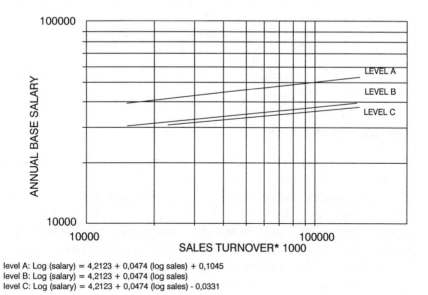

level A: Log (salary) = 4,2123 + 0,0474 (log sales) + 0,1045
level B: Log (salary) = 4,2123 + 0,0474 (log sales)
level C: Log (salary) = 4,2123 + 0,0474 (log sales) - 0,0331

Figure 5.4: *Product manager, annual base salary against company sales.*

Table 5.7: *Some examples of job summaries that Watson Wyatt uses in its survey*

Individuals covered: 86	D1	Q1	M	Q3	D9	A
Total sample characteristics						
Company sales	8	12	14	20	58	24
Company total employment	100	140	190	250	550	237
Job-holder's age	34	37	43	47	53	43
Years in present position	1	1	4	6	9	4

Direct compensation

All levels							
A + B + C	ABS	28462	31829	35307	40969	49865	37221
	ATR	33831	38716	49023	60262	65213	50088
Level A	ABS	32633	43749	49112	52511	56086	46672
	ATR	59833	60262	63653	65189	71310	63983
Level B	ABS	26113	31829	37506	40969	48972	36729
	ATR	29941	38716	47807	53158	56731	45693
Level C	ABS	28434	30853	32850	36548	39051	33562
	ATR	33831	35612	38397	39214	46391	38689

Director of marketing

The position reports direct to the Chief Executive with responsibility for initiating, planning, developing, co-ordinating and executing marketing policies and programmes, determining marketing opportunities and demand. May also have overseeing responsibilities for liaising with agents, market research, sales promotion, advertising, public relations and development of a marketing budget. If also responsible for direction of field sales force and the achievement of a sales target, the job should be matched against the Director of Sales.

Level A

The job-holder is responsible for marketing on an international scale or alternatively in a very large or diversified organisation. Would normally supervise a large team, either directly or indirectly, and have a key impact on company performance.

Level B

The job-holder heads up marketing for a domestic market in a large organisation. Would normally supervise a medium-sized team.

Level C

The job-holder heads up marketing in a smaller-sized operation. May supervise a small team of marketing support staff

Quality Control Manager

The position usually reports direct to the Director of Manufacturing and may also be called Quality Assurance Manager. Responsibility for overseeing all quality control procedures and implementing policies as directed by senior management to ensure conformity with legal or corporate specifications and standards. Supervises inspection and test-ing procedures and recommends corrective action as necessary.

Level A

The job-holder is responsible not only for quality control but also for quality assurance, ie anticipation of regulations and standards to be imposed in the future and initiating corrective action before mainline production activity commences. The product is usually highly sensi-tive (eg chemicals).

Level B

The job-holder heads up quality control in a large manufacturing operation, with full responsibility for all stages of the quality control activity. Likely to supervise a large team of quality inspectors, dealing with a technical product range.

Level C

The job-holder is responsible for quality control restricted to the final stage only, ie testing and discarding of substandard finished products. The job-holder may report to the Manufacturing Manager at this level.

6

Summary

Three groups of stakeholders in the organisation need to communicate on the remuneration policy and parts thereof. It becomes increasingly important that line management is well informed on all technical aspects of job evaluation and remuneration. Only then can it appreciate and approve the policy proposed. The personnel officer needs to master these technical aspects in order to develop sound proposals for this important element of personnel policy. The employees and their representatives need to agree with the proposed remuneration policy, which implies that they too must be familiar with the technical aspects and concepts.

The employees, their representatives (and in some European countries the official workers' council) are in general by no means experts on the subject. Employees need to form an opinion and agree with certain elements of the pay policy.

Frequently all parties lack knowledge of the various techniques discussed in this book, in spite of the fact that this knowledge is essential to arrive at sound judgements. The book has therefore explained, step by step, the technique of evaluating jobs and designing a salary structure.

Grading jobs and classifying job-holders demands insight into the elements that determine the weight of jobs. In addition, jobs in entirely different areas and disciplines need to be 'weighted' in relation to each other – a rather abstract and abstruse process. The way in which jobs are weighted is quite similar in most methods. Assessing the required knowledge or know-how, for instance, can be found in almost every method. How this characteristic of jobs is translated into a certain number of points has been demonstrated through a number of examples. Also, in methods in which jobs are 'weighted' by means of comparisons of job level descriptions, 'knowledge' is a major consideration in the evaluation. These methods, too, express the differences in know-how in to a number of points.

Some three (computerised) job evaluation methods have been compared, in each case using the treatment of 'knowledge' or 'know-how' as the main example, in addition to a characteristic that typifies the individual method. This approach provides, we expect, insight into the various versions on the one hand and into the similarities which, in principle, they all share on the other hand. A sound understanding of the characteristics for which a job is evaluated and weighted is very important. Only then will a personnel officer or consultant be able to draft a clear description of the so-called level indicators and sample summaries of jobs. These instruments are used in, for instance, a job level matrix. However, persons who are not responsible for the design of a job level matrix may also benefit from understanding these technical aspects. By developing a job level matrix the rigidity that surrounds job evaluation is broken up to a large degree. This is not only because the job level matrix lowers the threshold for grading and classifying jobs, but also because with the job evaluation matrix the organisation does not have to start from the existing situation and first carry out a so-called ascertaining job analysis. The job level matrix is a method of a rather normative nature, ie with this methodology tasks, responsibilities and account-abilities are considered from a logically coherent perspective of the organisation as a whole. The starting point is not what the job-holder does, but what he is supposed to do. The job-holder is evaluated for the degree in which he meets the job requirements; the method sets targets and objectives against which performance can be measured. The next logical step would be a structuring approach, in which a job is evaluated on the basis of the demands which the organisation sets in specific situations. It will be clear that such a structuring methodology will go back to the very rationale of the organisation. Why does the organisation exist? How can work in the organisation be divided and co-ordinated? The job level matrix fits excellently into this structuring approach.

Job evaluation needs not only to be more flexible in its design; it also needs to be smoothly linked with the remuneration policy. A change in the remuneration policy requires knowledge and insight into the underlying technique, so that a proper design can be made. This book provides the tools with which a salary structure can be designed and developed.

Rewarding is not simply setting a salary amount. The whole area of income in recent years has become more open for discussion. Individual salaries and salary scales used to be private or at least confidential issues. These days salary scales are more or less well known, depending upon the business or the organisation. Employees want to compare their classification to grades and pay lines. There are still only relatively few managers who know how a salary scale is built and what its components are. What are the rules? How do salary scales relate to the quality of life in the organisation? How can an enduring commitment to the organisation be made attractive?

Some organisations are best served by the traditional salary scale. It provides certainty to the employee, and the line manager is able simply to read off the scale the next salary amount to which an employee is entitled. However, in this way the responsibility for the remuneration of employees is not really being transferred to management. The 'open scales structure', which was discussed in Chapter 4 and which constitutes the basis for flexible salary structures, is a first step to shift this responsibility from the personnel department to the line manager. He will then have to explain differences in pay to both his subordinates and his superiors, especially if these differences are linked to the evaluation of employees.

If performance-related pay becomes an integrated element of the salary structure, a manager cannot any longer avoid assessing the performance of employees before he can decide on the real level of salaries. This causes an inherent conflict between the flexibility of the job evaluation and the traditional salary structure. Therefore, flexible remuneration structures are combined with the job level matrix in a new methodology.

Chapter 4 ended with a discussion on the so-called career remuneration model (CRM). This model offers flexibility in grading jobs and setting salaries. In setting performance-related pay levels the model makes a distinction between the qualitative and quantitative commitments underlying the achievements. In addition, it provides the opportunity to differentiate the remuneration in accordance with developments in the labour market.

With the CRM the added value an employee offers to the organisation can be rewarded. This added value is created when the employee acquires useful knowledge, skills or competencies which exceed the strict requirements of the job. At the same time the CRM can be used to manage the development of careers in terms of the salary both vertically and horizontally.

The model, however, also makes it possible to hire an employee at a lower grade (within the series of the job family) than fixed rules would prescribe. Arrangements concerning acquiring the skills to meet the job requirements and the assistance being offered can be made to provide clarity on the prospects.

Variations are conceivable and not all the possibilities of the CRM need to be exploited at once. Of course, flexibility of the remuneration policy is very much at the centre of attention. However, that does not mean that everyone knows how to take advantage of or even deal with this flexibility. The starting point of the remuneration policy should therefore always be the preconditions as they have been formulated by the organisation.

7

Definitions

Absolute maximum salary

Generally, this is the amount which an employee can reach when he performs 'very well' or 'outstandingly'. If a (limited) assessment or performance causes that salary to be higher than 100 per cent, then the sum of standard salary plus performance bonus is the absolute maximum salary.

Age-related pay

Within a specific grade the salary that is paid according to age.

Assessment increment

See Performance increment.

Base salary

Agreed standard salary plus (guaranteed) fixed remuneration components, such as a regional allowance, job supplements, guaranteed payments unrelated to performance, a fixed bonus, but excluding overtime, shift premiums, unsocial hours allowances. If other fixed components are part of the basic salary, the organisation needs to point this out explicitly in its salary survey questionnaire.

Benchmark job

A job that may serve as an example for a large number of jobs within, eg a certain function, trade, discipline, organisational unit or level, etc. Both parties, employer and employee, have agreed on the description and evaluation of the benchmark job.

Bonus

A once-only payment granted as a reward for extra effort. In some organisations agreements are made in advance on the level of effort.

Deciles/quartiles

D9: Upper or ninth decile

The upper or ninth decile represents the level at which 10 per cent of the observations have a score or value higher than that level and the other 90 per cent have a score or value lower than that level.

Q3: Upper or third quartile

The upper or third quartile represents the level at which 25 per cent of the observations have a score or value higher than that level and the other 75 per cent have a score or value lower than that level.

M: Median

The median represents the value of the middle observation.

A : Average

The average is the arithmetical middle of the values or scores of the observations.

Q1: Lower or first quartile

The lower or first quartile represents the level at which 75 per cent of the observations have a score or value lower than that level and the other 25 per cent have a score or value higher than that level.

D1: Lower or first decile

The lower or first decile represents the level at which 90 per cent of the observations have a score or value higher than that level and the other 75 per cent have a score of value lower than that level.

These concepts are illustrated in Figure 7.1.

Evaluation

Determining the relative weight of jobs, systematically using a weighing or measuring instrument.

General (initial) pay rise

This term refers to the increase of the basic salary that in principle every employee receives. Usually these increases are the outcome of (collective) negotiations with trade unions or other representatives of

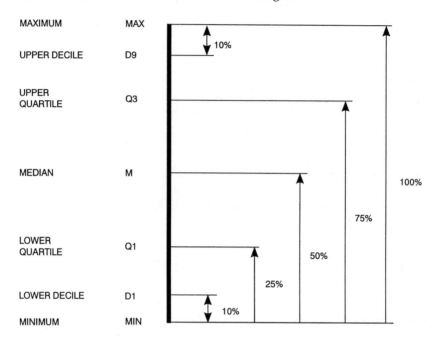

Figure 7.1: *Concepts of deciles and quartiles*

employees. The increment can be differentiated according to the weight and the hierarchical level of the job. If the increase is applied uniformly, it is nevertheless called an initial pay rise.

General once-only bonus

Such a bonus is usually the result of collective bargaining and has the form of a gross amount and/or a percentage of the basic salary. The actual payment is incidental and once only. In contrast to profit sharing and a bonus, it is not regarded as part of the basic salary.

Geometric scale

The difference between two consecutive values in a series is expressed as a percentage of the preceding value. For instance in the series, 100, 112, 136, 150 are transformed into the geometric scale of 1, 1.12, 1.21, 1.1.

Grade, job

A grade is a group of jobs which are accepted to be of a similar level and therefore receive a similar remuneration.

Grading

See Evaluating.

Individual increment

An added increase in salary to the general (initial) pay rise. This includes periodical increments or scale step increments, assessment increments and performance increments. Typically the level of the increment may vary for each employee. Also, in organisations that do not know general (initial) pay rises, an individual increment may mean the total rise in salary for each employee.

Increment

The amount by which the salary as a rule will be increased until the maximum salary of the grade is reached. The periodical increment is in general granted annually. See also Individual increment.

Initial salary rise

See General (initial) pay rise.

Job

A set of tasks which are linked to responsibilities and competencies.

Job analysis

The process by which the content of a job is analysed and relevant information for evaluating/grading of jobs is collected and recorded.

Job characteristic

Characteristic relevant for determining the level of a job. The content and importance of a job characteristic is defined by the job evaluation method.

Job description

A description of the job which is not exhaustive, but surveys the requirements and aspects of the job which are used in the job evaluation method and which provide insight into the factors which determine the weight of the job.

Job family

A number of jobs which are comparable in terms of content and techniques used. A job family can be grouped on the basis of a function or discipline (for instance, sales, accounting, production) on the one hand or on the basis of the nature of the work (for instance, secretarial jobs) on the other.

Job series

A series of jobs from the same job family which forms a logical sequence in terms of content and weight.

Line jobs

Jobs that are ultimately responsible and accountable for the output which a specific part of the organisation is expected to realise.

Logarithmic scale

The consecutive values of the scale are a factor 10 higher than its predecessor.

Maximum salary

The maximum salary that an employee obtains if he performs at a 'standard good' level. This maximum salary, sometimes called 'standard salary' or midpoint salary, is equated with 100 per cent; the individual salary, the minimum salary and the absolute maximum salary are expressed as a percentage of this maximum salary. The standard salary (100 per cent) can be taken as the benchmark of the comparisons.

Metrical scale

The consecutive values on a scale have equal distances to each other. An example is the length of a yardstick.

Midpoint

The midpoint of a grade is the salary amount that every employee reaches if he carries out his job normally. In terms of the weight of a job the midpoint is the middle of the grade, expressed in job evaluation points.

Minimum salary

The starting salary for an adult employee in a specific grade or salary scale. In general only salaries for young employees may be lower than this minimum salary.

Points range

The limits of a grade, usually expressed in job evaluation points, by which jobs of a similar level are grouped.

Overlap

The difference between the maximum salary of a grade x and the minimum salary of the next higher grade $x + 1$.

Pay line (within the same salary band)

Line along which the salary of an individual progresses to its assigned maximum in the salary band based on assessment of his performance.

Pay policy line

The line connecting the midpoint salaries or, in some organisations, the maximum salaries of consecutive grades.

Pay practice line

The line indicating the relationship between, for instance, the total score of job evaluation points and the factually paid full-time salaries. Instead of job evaluation points another measure can be used as well. The line representing this statistical relationship is also called the regression line.

Pay range

The difference between minimum and maximum salary within a salary band.

Performance increment

See Performance-related pay.

Performance-related pay

The (extra) remuneration that an employee receives as a reward for recognisably higher performances than can be expected if a job is carried out normally. In general this remuneration is determined as a percentage of the scale salary and is granted as long as the higher performances are realised. Sometimes an amount of money will be paid afterwards for extra efforts during a certain period. This form of performance-related pay is sometimes called a bonus.

Progression in a salary scale

The difference between the level of salaries in consecutive grades. The progression is usually expressed as a percentage of the difference between maximum salary amounts.

Prospects

The distance between the factual salary and the maximum of the grade in which the employee has been classified. Prospects may also refer to the opportunities for progress of an employee's salary through various grades (for instance, as a result of a re-evaluation of his job).

Ranking

Putting jobs in the order of their increasing weight, expressed in a total number of job evaluation points.

Remuneration policy

The series of standard salaries or midpoint salaries which have been established for the consecutive grades or scales. The 'pay policy line', which is formed by this series of standard or midpoint salaries, can be used for external comparisons. The 'pay practice line' is determined in the same manner provided that instead of the standard or midpoint salary the corresponding factual salaries are taken.

Salary band

The area which is formed by the salaries of jobs of similar level (job grade). A coherent set of (salary) bands is called a salary scale.

Salary practice

The (gross) salary that is periodically paid to a full-time employee. The limits for this salary are usually set by the minimum and the absolute maximum salaries. See Pay practice line.

Salary rise, across the board

This refers to the increase in salary that applies in principle to all employees.

Salary rise, promotion

The increase in salary as a result of the employee being assigned to a heavier job which is assigned to a higher grade.

Salary scale

A set of (salary) amounts which are systematically linked to each other. A salary scale consists of several grades.

Salary scale amount

The amount of salary between the minimum and maximum salary of a grade assigned to an employee. In the traditional salary structure the amount of the salary is linked to a scale step.

Salary structure

The mutual 'technical' relationship on which a salary scale rests. The technical relationship is the set of parameters that determines the amounts of salaries in the salary scale.

Scale step

The serial number referring to a fixed amount somewhere between the minimum salary (scale step 0) and the maximum salary (scale step x).

Supporting positions

Jobs that are created to provide specialist knowledge in a certain field and have the task of supporting line management in developing and implementing policies and making decisions.

System formula

The formula which defines the relationship between the remuneration levels within a series of consecutive grades.

System-holder

The organisation which owns the job evaluation method and is therefore responsible for a correct application of that method.

Task

A set of similar or corresponding activities.

Total cash

Total cash is the basic salary plus all variable (non-guaranteed) remuneration components. It excludes all forms of costs allowances because these components are not formally part of the remuneration. Examples of variable remuneration are: bonuses, profit-sharing, gain sharing, emoluments, etc.

Weighing factors

Multipliers in a job evaluation method with which the relative value of a job characteristic can be expressed.

Width of grade

See Job ... headings.

Appendix 1

Request for a job analysis

To: Personnel Department _____
From: Head/chief of department/function/unit _____
Date: _____

I request that an analysis be made of the following job of which:

☐ no job description has been made (*new job*)

☐ a job description has already been made (*existing job*)

New job

☐ The job has not yet been filled

☐ The job is/will be carried out by:

Name: _____

Department/unit: _____

The tasks of the job are/will be carried out under the direct supervision of:

Name : _____

Department/unit: _____

Existing job

The job is being carried out by job-holder:

Name: _____

Department/unit: _____

Job title/name: _____

Job code: _____

In the current conditions the existing job description does not reflect the job content any longer, due to the following reasons:

_____

_____

Applicant's signature _____

Appendix 2

Request for bringing an appeal against the results of a job evaluation

Name: _____

Department/unit: _____

Job title/name: _____

Job code: _____

Contents of the appeal
(Clearly indicate whether the appeal is against the content of the job description or against the grading or assignment of the job. If possible, indicate whether data are omitted, errors are made in the job description, or the grading, or assignment of the job is in your opinion not correct in view of the grading/assignment of other jobs. Please indicate why you think so.)

Signature _____ Date _____

Any comments by superior
(The superior is expected to give an opinion not only on the complaint as such, but also on the reasons for the complaint having been brought forward.)

Signature_____ Date _____

Comments by Personnel Department
(Conclusions, decisions, arrangements, etc.)

_____

_____

_____

Dealt with by: _____

To be considered and filled out after the complaints have been dealt with by the Personnel Department.

The employee asks to submit his complaint before the supervising commission:

☐ Yes   ☐ No

The employee asks to be given an opportunity to explain his complaint in person before the commission of appeal.

☐ Yes   ☐ No

To be considered and filled out after the complaint is treated by the commission.

The employee requests to submit his complaint before the commission of appeals:

☐ Yes   ☐ No

The commission of appeals is requested to record its findings in writing and to attach these to this form.

General

Received by Personnel Department: _____

Received by commission of appeals: _____

The job will be reassigned to/remains to be assigned to grade: _____

Appellant/complainant informed on (date): _____

Appendix 3

Rules for review and appeal

Section 1

The job-holder may only request a review of the results of a job evaluation after being informed by the Head of the Personnel Department of these results and of the position of the job in question relative to similar jobs.

Section 2

The request for a review must be made in writing by the job-holder, must state the reasons why a review should be made and must be submitted to the Head of the Personnel Department within two months after the date on which the job-holder has been informed in writing of the results of the job evaluation.

Section 3

Paragraph 1
The request for a review must be treated by the supervising commission of the evaluation project. If possible, a decision should be taken within three months after the request has been submitted. The job-holder/complainant must be informed of that decision and the reasons in writing.

Paragraph 2
An appeal against the decision of the supervising commission may be brought before the commission of appeals, in writing within two months. Before taking a decision the commission of appeals will give the supervising commission an opportunity to be heard. During the discussions on the appeal a member of the supervising commission may be present.

Paragraph 3

If possible the commission of appeals will decide on the appeal within three months after the submission of the written appeal and state the reasons for this decision.

Section 4

If, as a consequence of a review or a decision of the commission of appeals, a job is re-evaluated and assigned to a different grade, any salary adjustment will be backdated over the period during which the salary should have been paid according to the review or the decision of the commission.

This appeal procedure only applies to internal appeals. In some cases there will be a need to have a procedure for appeals before an external body, for instance before a joint committee of employers and trade unions.

In addition to the procedure for the implementation of job evaluation and for bringing appeals, many organisations create a supervisory commission. The task of such a commission is to supervise the correct and timely implementation of the agreed procedures and to advise parties involved if asked.

For the proper functioning of that commission it is recommended that rules and regulations are drafted in which the composition, objectives, tasks and competence, etc are settled. An example of such rules and regulations is provided in Appendix 4.

Appendix 4

Rules and regulations for Supervising Commission for job evaluation

Section 1: Definitions

In these rules and regulations the following definitions apply:

- Company: Fiction Publishing Limited
- Management: Board of Directors and Managing Director of Fiction Publishing Limited
- Commission: Supervising Commission for job evaluation
- Experts: Specialists appointed by the Company who on its behalf carry out the job evaluation project

Section 2: Appointment of the Commission

2.1 A Supervising Commission will be appointed for the duration of the job evaluation project. The number of members of the Commission will depend upon the size of the company, respectively of the subsidiary.

2.2 The members of the Commission will be partly selected from representatives of the employees concerned and partly appointed by the management. In addition, the members selected by the employees and appointed by the management will jointly appoint one of the specialists carrying out the project as an adviser to the Commission. The Commission will be resolved at the end of the job evaluation project.

2.3 If a member withdraws from the Commission, the party which that member represented selects or appoints a new member within two months.

2.4 The members of the Commission must be mature in their discipline, or trade and have been in the employment of the company for at least two years. The members of the Commission must be prepared to take part in a special training programme.

2.5 Membership of the Commission ends:
- after the job evaluation project is completed;
- when leaving the employment of the company;
- by resigning;
- if the representatives of the employees and the management jointly decide to end the membership of a person on the grounds that he or she does not act in accordance with the spirit of co-operation necessary for achieving the objectives of the project.

Section 3: Purpose of the Commission

To supervise and monitor the preparation, implementation and completion of the job evaluation project and the procedures it requires in such a way that acceptance of and adherence to the results by the employees involved is as wide as possible.

Section 4: Duties and competencies of the Commission

4.1 The Commission will monitor and support the preparation, implementation and completion of the job evaluation project with regard to the methods, procedures, planning and progress. It promotes the communication of effective information on the system and its techniques to the employees concerned. The Commission contributes to the smooth progress of the project by preventing, signalling or rectifying misunderstandings and incorrect information.

4.2 The Commission performs a monitoring/advisory role in dealing with complaints about procedures and/or differences of opinion between the employee concerned, his departmental head and/or experts with regard to the job descriptions. In doing so it will not interfere with the authority of the management of the department.

4.3 The Commission forms an opinion on the preparatory job ranking the experts have made as a basis for comparisons. It may advise the experts to carry out further investigations if it cannot agree with this job ranking. The experts remain ultimately responsible for the final ranking of jobs which will be presented to the management.

4.4 The Commission has access to all data and records which may provide insight into the implementation process and must be informed about complaints regarding this process in order to make an independent and objective judgement. The information provided must be kept confidential.

4.5 The Commission is competent to hear the parties involved in disputes and to obtain advice from third parties.

4.6 Proposals for changes in the approach, implementation, procedures, planning, etc of the project can be submitted to the Commission by its members, the Personnel Department and the experts. Its decisions are binding for the parties concerned in so far as these recognise the competence and responsibility of the management of the department and of the system-holder.

Section 5: Rules for the meetings of the Commission

5.1 The Commission appoints a chairman from its members.

5.2 The Commission meets at least once every two months or more frequently if required in the course of the project.

5.3 The Commission may invite experts to attend its meeting.

Section 6: Confidentiality

6.1 The members of the Commission and its advisers are to keep confidential all information they obtain in their capacity as members or advisers of the Commission, unless explicitly stated differently.

6.2 The pledge of confidentiality is not removed by terminating the membership of the Commission for whatever reasons.

Section 7: Protection

The management of the company ensures that the members of the Commission will not be infringed in their rights, or put at a disadvantage in their position in the company, as a result of their membership of the Commission.

Section 8: Interpretation of and changes in these rules and regulations

8.1 In case of disputes on the application and interpretation of these rules and regulations the management and a delegation of the employees decide jointly after hearing the parties concerned.

8.2 These rules and regulations can be changed or supplemented by a joint decision of the management and delegates of the employees.

Appendix 5

Questionnaire for job analysis

As was pointed out earlier, the questionnaire is an excellent instrument for collecting relevant information on the jobs to be analysed. It is also very useful as a preparation for the interview with the job analyst. The structure of the questionnaire should match the job evaluation method that will be used. In addition, the format of the questionnaire should be such that it collects sufficient information on both operational and staff jobs. It is recommended that a short explanation be given on each question. The following example contains the essence of the questionnaires used by the Hay method.

Name of the company: ....

Name of the sector/department: ....

Name of the job-holder: ....

Reports to (job title): ....

Date: ....

Organisation chart

Please draw an 'organisation chart' which clearly indicates the position of your job. Indicate whether subordinate jobs report to your job and if so, which jobs report to the same immediate superior as yours. Also, stipulate any relationships with another functional job. In the organisation chart use a full line for hierarchical relationships and a dotted line for functional relationships.

Relevant quantitative information

Please indicate some of the areas which your job influences directly or indirectly. Quantify the areas which your job influences as far as possible in terms of numbers, amounts, percentages, etc. In Table A.5.1 you will find some examples.

Table A.5.1: *Quantitative information*

	Last year	This year	In three years' time
Number of subordinates			
Annual sales			
Costs budget			
Labour costs			
Value added			
Capital investment budget			

What are the major activities?

What are the main activities expected from you? In addition to 'what', please indicate 'why'.

Summary of the functional area

Please give a short summary of your job and of the area in which its activities are. You should consider issues such as: type and nature of work and activities; the most important characteristics of the functional area; the features and characteristics that distinguish this area from other functional areas within the organisation, etc.

Communication skills/human resource skills

Please indicate the major internal and external contacts and relationships that you, in the capacity of your job, need to maintain. Specify the function/department/organisation with which you maintain relationships and describe the nature and the purpose of these contacts. Give an estimation of the frequency of these contacts.

In the capacity of your job you may be a member of one or more commissions and councils. Of which major bodies are you a member by virtue of this job? What is your role in these bodies? List the names of these bodies, their nature and purpose and the frequency with which they meet.

Do you have to use a foreign language in your job?

Specific questions

Functional accountability

Please indicate the jobs from which you receive immediate instructions and assignments and on which your immediate superior has no authority, as in projects, or in some of your tasks as a specialist. Give a short description of the nature and purpose of these activities.

Hierarchical leadership

In your job are you in charge of subordinate employees?

If so, please list these jobs, give a short description of the results that are expected of these jobs and what your contribution is towards achieving these results.

Functional leadership

Please list any other (non-subordinate) employees to whom you give direct instructions and assignments and on which the immediate hierarchical superior has no authority, such as in projects in specialist activities, and give a short description of the nature and purpose of these jobs.

Complexity of issues

What is the nature of the problems and issues you need to solve? What is the nature of the solutions expected from you?

Specific problems

Give two controversial issues for which a solution is expected from you.

Instructions and constraints

With which rules and constraints do you have to comply in carrying out your job? (For instance, prices, discounts, budgets, systems, codes, reports, procedures, etc.) Which decisions do you have to submit to your direct superior?

Specific skills

Do you have to operate special equipment?

Do you have to work or process specific materials? If so, which?

Does your job demand special attention, accuracy or precision? If so, in what sense?

Are special faculties required (smell, taste, distinguishing colours, etc)? If so, which?

Accountablities

Specify the main results which you are expected to achieve. We do not want you to describe the various duties and activities, but are looking for a concise summary of the main results. What are your main responsibilities? What levels must be attained?

Objective of the job

Please try to describe briefly and concisely (in one or two sentences) the objective of your job. What does it contribute to the organisation as a whole; what is the share of your results in the total activities?

Inconveniences

Does your job include activities which require physical force? If so, which?

Does your job include activities which require an unnatural, forced position? If so, which?

In your job do you run the risk of catching a disease or having an accident?

In this questionnaire other items can be included as well, depending on the job evaluation method used. These differences are not essential, but may assist in the ranking of a job or in subdividing the 'characteristics' which the method uses in to 'factors/aspects'. It is recommended that the questionnaire should start with detailed questions of the job and gradually progress to the final descriptions of the objectives and responsibilities of the job.

The above questionnaire includes items which are typical for jobs of a supporting or advisory nature (staff jobs); other items apply more to operational activities. It may be sensible to draft one questionnaire for both categories of jobs and then make a specialised questionnaire for certain groups of jobs.

Appendix 6

Business characteristics of Fiction Publishing Limited
(basic document for the Personnel Department)

History

Fiction Publishing Limited was founded in 1948. Its original business was to publish school books for primary education. After a number of take-overs of smaller companies between 1981 and 1982 its activities were substantially extended. In the mid-eighties the publishing company had a comprehensive list of titles intended for higher professional education and for practising professionals of an advanced level. Because of its strong position in both market segments, the company was bought by the publishing corporation INFO in 1990.

Main activity

Fiction Publishing Limited produces (intellectually and technically) and markets high-level educational and informational publishing products, in particular in the field of marketing, personnel, social law, and insurance and pensions.

The products are distributed by a sister company (Distrifiction).

Organisation structure

The organisation structure is market-oriented and product/market departments have been separated from supporting departments. The product/market departments are business units which are responsible for sales and profit margin. These departments are headed by a Head of Publishing Department (see Figure A.6.1). Together these heads of departments form the so-called executive team, which is chaired by the managing director. In total, Fiction Publishing employs some 280 persons.

The primary functional areas are as follows:

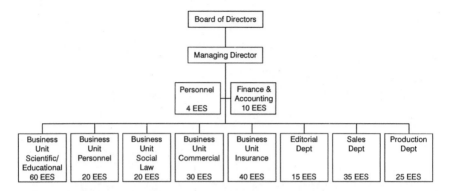

Figure A.6.1: *Main organisation structure of the company*

Publishing department

The objective of the publishing department is to develop and realise products and series of products which transfer targeted information to specific market segments. This should be done on a commercial basis in a way which ensures the continuity of the company and contributes to achieving its long-term and short-term objectives. At an operational level this involves shared responsibility for the systematic development of products that meet the information needs of the target market segment. This requires:

– developing a strategic plan for the publishing departments, which focus on long-term objectives in terms of return on investment and market share, taking into account trends and developments in the market;
– drafting an annual budget, a marketing plan and a budget for developing, producing and marketing (new) products;
– monitoring trends and developments in the relevant markets and collecting and interpreting marketing information in order to find new opportunities for further growth of market shares;
– implementing the plans, managing the budget and realising the expected contribution to sales and profits; after consulting the marketing department, formulating capital investment plans for new markets, publishing projects, marketing programmes, design of products, etc.

Editorial department

Main tasks of the editorial staff are editing and styling manuscripts and preparing these manuscripts for production and printing.

Trade-offs must be made between preparation and production costs on the one hand and the wishes of publishers and authors as well as technical features on the other. The editorial staff is responsible for a balanced distribution of text and illustrations and for the structure and logical progress of texts, while ensuring the maintenance and enhancement of the publishing style of the company and checking texts on spelling and references. The editorial staff represents the company in dealing with authors and co-ordinates editorial tasks, production and marketing. In addition, it monitors and manages the costs of publishing projects.

Sales department

The tasks and responsibilities of the sales department include:

- implementing the marketing plan, which should result in growth in market share, successful sales of publishing products and improved profitability;
- improving the market position of the business units through market research, drafting proposals concerning product/market combinations and marketing programmes for market (segments);
- developing sales plans for products and services of the company and initiating, implementing and co-ordinating promotional programmes;
- systematically enhancing the relationships between the business units and their target groups through public relations and marketing communication.

Production department

The objectives and tasks of the production department are:

- planning, implementing and managing the transformation process from manuscript into a final publishing product. The process includes designing illustrations, purchasing, printing and bookbinding services, and lithos and paper from third parties. The production department is responsible for budgeting and costing projects.
- requesting bids for annual purchasing needs, assessing the technical features, quality and prices of bids by suppliers, preparing purchasing contracts.
- keeping well informed of and advising the business units on technical developments, databases, new media, publishing software, etc.

Finance and Accounting department

The main objective of the department Finance and Accounting is to create and improve financial conditions and management information systems which the company requires to achieve its short-term and long-term objectives. This involves:

- supporting the development of strategic plans and the translation of these plans into annual plans and budgets;
- advising on financial and accounting issues (acquisitions, reorganisation, studies, external business information);
- designing and maintaining an appropriate accounting system, including a financial accounting system and a management information system, which provide accurate and timely financial statements and reports for managing the business operations and the financial position of the company;
- managing the financial resources of the company;
- ensuring compliance with accounting standards (internal control);
- providing information and computer services in support of company objectives.

Personnel department

The main objective of the decentralised Personnel Department is to create or to contribute to personnel and organisation conditions which effectively and efficiently support achieving the long- and short-term objectives of the company. This requires:

- integrating the personnel policy into the overall policy and strategy of the corporation as a whole and the company in such a way that balances the capabilities, expectations, wants and interests of the people in the company with its financial and commercial objectives;
- designing and implementing the personnel policy which is supported by an integrated system of (personnel) management instruments and systems for personnel development and coaching;
- (participating in) developing the structure of the organisation;
- in consultation with line managers carrying out advisory, supporting, operational and controlling activities in the area of personnel management;
- developing and implementing the personnel administration.

Products and market

The company's main products, delivery systems and markets are summarised in Figure A.6.2.

The conventional printed periodicals are distributed by mail in frequencies ranging from fortnightly to bimonthly. The one-off publications are supplementary to the various periodicals.

Currently, the emphasis in both publishing and organising conferences is on employment and labour law and industrial relations, with health and safety being the only field of real growth. As a consequence of this subject area, the market of the company is primarily the UK (85 per cent of sales).

Until 1989 the development of products/market was incidental and evolved exclusively from the company's publishing activities. In the

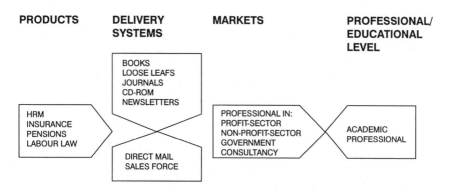

Figure A.6.2: *Market shares*

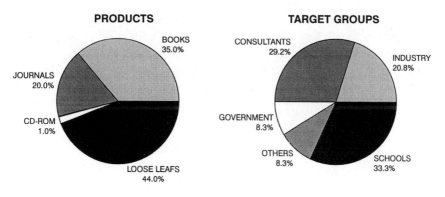

Figure A.6.3: *Market shares*

four years since the company was acquired by the INFO Group, only two new titles were developed and launched.

In the new company strategy currently being developed, a more systematic approach towards new product development and acquisitions will be adopted. As a first step in this strategy a rigorous evaluation will be made of the current market position and opportunities for future growth in the key markets. The new strategy, however, cannot be fully implemented until the new editorial structure has been completed (next budget period) and the forthcoming arrival of a new marketing manager who has been selected for his knowledge and skills in market research.

Production process

The contents of the majority of the Fiction publications have been produced internally by the editorial and research staff. Feature contributions and in-depth case studies are written after extensive research, including interviews and written exchanges with a wide range of influential sources in industry, government, trade unions, employers' confederations and also with academics. Producing these texts requires a combination of skills, command of the art and techniques of investigative journalism, plus subject expertise and thorough research skills and a close proximity to the information sources, who in many cases are also subscribers. Accuracy, credibility and diplomacy are essential requirements.

In addition to writing feature contributions and checking their contents with external sources, the production process includes the following steps:

- Editorial planning. This generates themes for future feature contributions, case studies and in-depth investigative reports.
- Interviews with key sources by researchers/editors who then create a built-up story and check with advisers and other contacts.
- Editorial copy. This is written and edited – for style and length – by a production editor.
- Marking up and preparing copy for external typesetting by the production department.
- Typeset copy is made proof-ready by the production department and editorial staff.
- Corrected copy is reset, pages are agreed and copy is sent to printers.

– Printed volumes are sent direct from printers to subscribers and buyers on the basis of mailing lists supplied by the sales department.

The editorial production process includes in-house keyboarding (on typewriters or microcomputers) and re-keying and typesetting. Negotiations are under way with editors' trade unions to prepare for the automation of the editorial production process and the elimination of re-keying. Currently little advantage is taken of the state-of-the-art technology, but it is envisaged that in the near future the entire process will be completely 're-engineered'.

With high frequency publications and labour intensive production processes, schedules are tight and people are always working under pressure. Some internal cost rates are set high, emphasising the need for quality and fast cycle times.

Research and development costs and investments are not traced separately, but are included in the general marketing and editorial budgets. It is estimated that R & D consumes less than 1.5 per cent of gross sales. This situation is similar to that of competitors.

As can be expected with the close relationships between editorial staff and subscribers, the most effective sales channel is direct marketing, ie orders received in response to direct mail promotions.

Depending upon the market segment, the list of publications and the individual product, Fiction Publishers Limited uses a variety of marketing and sales techniques: premium offers, price reductions, trial offers and sample copies. One of its main challenges is to continue to find new approaches for a mature market. This challenge is the more important as sales to cross subscribers is the most cost-effective approach in the business.

In its markets for professionals Fiction Publishing Limited's pricing is a difficult and continuous problem for which there are no simple answers. Due to a lack of research into price elasticity, pricing is unsystematic and not scientific and therefore tends to be rather conservative.

The major components of the cost price of products are:

Periodicals	Printing/typesetting/paper
	Distribution
	Fees for external editorial contributions
	Editorial staff
	Marketing/sales promotion

    Conferences   Location/speakers
                           Staff
                           Marketing/promotion

More than a quarter of total sales is generated by publications and one quarter by conferences.

Table A.6.4: *Strategic issues*

Basic financial figures

Profit and loss account	1996	2000
Total sales	45.0	51.0
Value added	4.5	6.0
Operating profit	2.0	2.8
Balance sheet		
Total assets	40.0	45.0
Capital employed	11.0	12.0
Working capital	13.0	19.0
Number of employees	250	280

Strategic issues

This part of the business characteristics provides details of the SWOT analysis (see Table A.6.4).

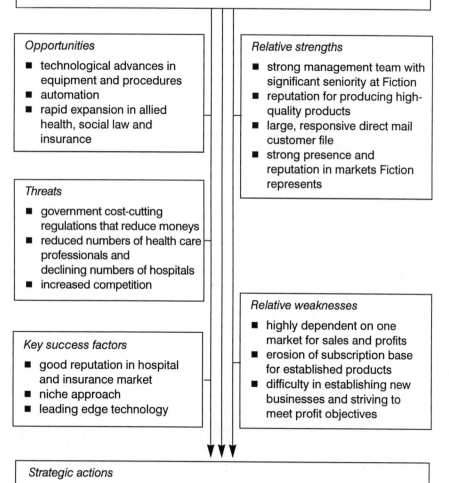

Corporate objectives

a significant amount of effort will be focused on profit improvement to increase the operating income to 12 per cent of sales within the next 3 years

to invest in (electronic) products and product lines that offer the highest profit opportunities and cutting back in those areas that have been growing more slowly and take a maintenance level posture

to build subscription business

Opportunities

- technological advances in equipment and procedures
- automation
- rapid expansion in allied health, social law and insurance

Relative strengths

- strong management team with significant seniority at Fiction
- reputation for producing high-quality products
- large, responsive direct mail customer file
- strong presence and reputation in markets Fiction represents

Threats

- government cost-cutting regulations that reduce moneys
- reduced numbers of health care professionals and declining numbers of hospitals
- increased competition

Key success factors

- good reputation in hospital and insurance market
- niche approach
- leading edge technology

Relative weaknesses

- highly dependent on one market for sales and profits
- erosion of subscription base for established products
- difficulty in establishing new businesses and striving to meet profit objectives

Strategic actions

- carefully balancing new products development and growth especially in electronic products with investment in existing products
- steady sales growth
- to move away from the reliance on health administration and to grow and rapidly expand in allied health, insurance, social law
- establishing a presence in the law market

Appendix 7

Company: Fiction Publishing Limited
Department: Sales
Job title: Secretary

Purpose of the job:

Providing, in effective and efficient ways, full secretarial support to the head and staff of the department so that they are able to carry out their tasks, using the available time and resources as efficiently as possible.

Organisation chart

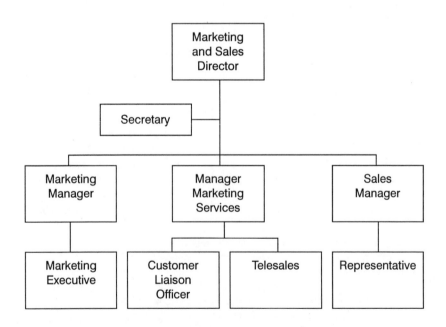

Figure A.7.1: *Organisation chart sales department*

Relevant quantitative information:

Sales 1995 : _____

Departmental budget :_____

Relevant accountabilities: _____

Communication

Ensuring efficient internal communication, in particular recording and passing through messages and appointments.

Core activities:

- accepting, (if possible, screening) and passing through incoming calls for head and staff;
- dealing with routine issues (such as providing information on the basis of available data);
- keeping an office diary, co-ordinating and monitoring appointments of head and staff;
- making hotel reservations and travel bookings on the basis of instructions/wishes of the head and staff.

Correspondence

Effectively processing and recording business information and arrangements.

Core activities:

- selecting incoming and outgoing mail for head and staff;
- screening the main distribution to head and staff;
- handling the correspondence of the department on the basis of guidelines and instructions;
    - taking notes and drafting letters and reports, which may be of a technical or confidential nature;
    - independently handling routine correspondence which need not be submitted to the head of staff (eg acknowledgements, appointments, information, documentation);
    - drafting letters and presenting them for signature by head or staff;
    - checking and correcting texts for style and spelling.

Information processing and management

Information which is available and accessible to head and staff.

Core activities:

- managing the mail and documentation files, which include confidential material;
- providing data to others upon request of head or staff;
- requesting information from internal/external sources upon request of head or staff;
- collecting and processing data on the basis of clear instructions;
- collecting data for meetings, distributing documents according to instructions, taking notes and making a first draft of minutes or reports, submitting these drafts for approval and distributing the minutes;
- drafting special documents according to clear instructions of head.

Miscellaneous

Providing accurate support for specific tasks of department.

Core activities:

- welcoming and attending to visitors;
- dealing with standard administrative tasks related to secretarial work.

Appendix 8

Company: Fiction Publishing Limited
Department: Personnel
Job title: Head of Personnel

Purpose of the job

Developing and, after approval, implementing and managing the company's long-term and short-term policy concerning personnel and organisation, including the personnel management instruments, in such a way that an effective and efficient labour organisation is built and maintained at acceptable costs.

Organisation chart

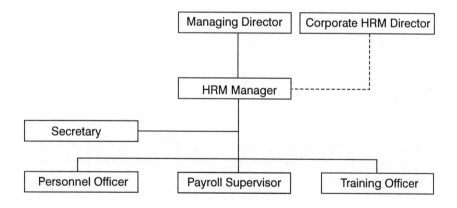

Figure A.8.1: *Organisation chart personnel department.*

Relevant quantitative information

Number of employees: _____

Total amount of wages: _____

Training budget: _____

Sales: _____

Relevant accountabilities:

Personnel policy

Approved personnel policy for the organisation including principles, guidelines and procedures for personnel management aimed at optimum deployment of employees.

Core activities:

– monitoring developments in medium-term plans of the company, keeping well informed of personnel issues in general, of relevant laws and regulations and of trends in labour markets;
– translating this information into implications for personnel and personnel management within the company;
– developing and adjusting (elements of) personnel policy;
– obtaining approval of management for personnel policy.

Annual plan and budget

Approved annual plan and budget for activities concerning personnel issues within the company, which specifies objectives, programmes, activities and available resources for the coming year within the context of the corporate and company medium-term plans.

Core activities:

– translating the approved medium-term plans into targets to be realised within the coming year;
– drafting an annual activities plan including a costs budget, which looks forward to the years ahead;
– submitting the annual plan of the budget for approval.

Terms of employment

Developing and obtaining approval of a package of employment conditions and terms that are competitive and in proper proportion to the various jobs of differing weight in the company.

Core activities:

- monitoring and ensuring the correct application of the job evaluation method; monitoring the relative positions and weights of jobs as a basis for developing a package of employment terms and conditions;
- keeping abreast of developments in the market concerning employment terms for exempted and non-exempted jobs;
- analysing the position of the company in the labour markets on the basis of information from salary surveys;
- drawing the attention of the corporate labour relations department to issues to be considered in collective bargaining;
- making proposals regarding the elements of the package of employment terms for various groups of jobs and obtaining approval from corporate Personnel function.

Recruitment, selection and departure

Effective methods for the recruitment and selection of candidates for vacant positions in the company and for employees who are leaving, which support the decisions of line management and enhance the continuity in the occupation of positions.

Core activities:

- investigating the present and future quantitative and qualitative manpower requirements;
- profiling the company in the labour market; maintaining relationships with labour markets;
- implementing recruitment activities, including arranging personnel advertisements;
- monitoring and ensuring the uniform application of selection and dismissal procedures by line managers;
- upon request of line management, supporting and advising on the selection process;
- reporting deviations of employment terms to top management and the corporate Personnel Function and, if necessary, arranging personality and aptitude tests;
- drafting letters of appointment/dismissal and having these signed by top management;
- designing and implementing or having implemented the introduction and trial programmes;

- concluding, managing and monitoring contracts with employment agencies for temporary personnel; monitoring the observance of these contracts by line management;
- co-signing the employment contracts of temporary employees and monitoring the compliance with legal requirements concerning dismissals.

Assessment

Effective methods for assessing employees in support of line management and aimed at insight into the quality of personnel.

Core activities:

- monitoring and ensuring the (uniform) application of assessment procedures by line management;
- initiating and supervising the annual assessment cycle as a basis for adjustment of employment terms, training programmes and career planning;
- upon request of line management of employees, providing support and advice on the assessment process;
- signalling and reporting to top management deviations and abnormalities in completed assessments.

Training

Effective approach and organisation of training programmes for employees aimed at optimising the work organisation on long and short term.

Core activities:

- monitoring and ensuring the (uniform) application of training procedures by line management;
- taking stock of the training needs and wishes of employees and giving advice;
- maintaining contacts with external training institutes;
- organising training in company courses in collaboration with line management.

Management development and career planning

Effective approach and implementation of management development and career planning aimed at enhancing the long-term continuity of the publishing company in terms of a qualitatively sound occupation of management positions, now and in the future.

Core activities:

- taking stock of the demands and requirements of future management positions within the company;
- assessing (or having assessed) the required and available potential within the company/corporation;
- assessing (or having assessed) career wishes of employees;
- drafting proposals for top management for adjustments or general measures if the required future potential and talent is not available;
- ensuring the implementation of approved measures, if necessary in collaboration with corporate staff Management Development.

Terms of employment/legal regulations

Correct and adequate terms of employment and working conditions, including programmes for health and safety, in accordance with the collective labour contracts and laws, government regulations and adequate programmes for sick employees.

Core activities:

- keeping abreast of developments in laws and regulations concerning employment, safety and health and workers' participation;
- implementing measures to comply with these laws and regulations;
- maintaining contacts with trade unions and employees' representatives;
- keeping in contact with sick employees, providing for re-entry facilities and arrangements after recovering;

Management reporting

Periodic management reports on personnel issues (quantitative and qualitative data) according to established (corporate) guidelines which can be used as steering information by management.

Core activities:

- operating the personnel information system (personal files of employees, sickness, turnover, etc);
- periodically collecting relevant information concerning personnel issues;
- drafting, explaining and presenting management reports to top management.

Appendix 9

EC CODE OF PRACTICE
COMMISSION OF THE EUROPEAN COMMUNITIES

Brussels, 17.07.1996
COM(96) 336 final

INFORMATION CONCERNING A CODE OF PRACTICE ON THE IMPLEMENTATION OF EQUAL PAY FOR WORK OF EQUAL VALUE FOR WOMEN AND MEN WITHIN THE EUROPEAN COMMUNITY

INTRODUCTION

The principle of equal pay for men and women for work of equal value is based on Article 119 of the Treaty of Rome and on the 1975 directive relating to the application of the principle of equal pay for men and women[1].

Despite these provisions of Community law having been adopted and transposed into the legislations of the Member States 20 years ago, the differences in pay between women and men remain considerable.

What is more, it is confirmed that these pay differences are even greater for non-manual than they are for manual workers, which reflects the many different types of job available and the tendency for men to occupy managerial positions and women to be secretaries, whereas in the case of manual workers, the distribution of jobs, and therefore of pay is more restricted.

The difference between women and men's incomes is due to many factors and in particular:

– to the vertical and horizontal segregation of jobs held by women and men (so-called female jobs are still generally less well paid),
– to the numerous sectors of the economy where mainly men work, offering extra pay, working time bonuses etc, all of which widen the pay disparities between the sectors outside of the base rates,
– to the considerable differentiation in pay resulting from collective agreements linked to the recognition of skills, to the type of business and the type of industry or sector. Gender-specific segregation in employment applies to each of these divisions, increasing the potential for such differentiation,
– to the systems of collective agreements which allow salary structures to reflect the negotiating power of different groups of employees. As a result, women are generally weaker in negotiations.

[1]Directive (EEC) N. 75/117 of the Council OJ N. L 45, 19.2.1975, p.19

In order to help lessen this difference, the Commission has decided to adopt this code of practice which follows on from its Memorandum on Equal Pay for Work of Equal Value, published in June 1994[2].

The Code aims to provide *concrete advice* for employers and collective bargaining partners at business, sectoral or intersectoral level to ensure that the principle of equality between women and men performing work of equal value is applied to all aspects of pay. In particular it aims to eliminate sexual discrimination whenever pay structures are based on job classification and evaluation systems.

The nature of the approaches and measures set out in the Code is neither exhaustive nor legally binding but provides models for action which could be taken in the area in question. The Code should be read in conjunction with the memorandum, which illustrates the principle of equal pay in the light of the decisions of the Court of Justice of the European Communities.

Codes of practice are more widely and effectively applied when they have been conceived in close co-operation with the intended users. This is why the Commission consulted the social partners on the content and drafting of the current code. It was essential for the Code to reflect, as far as possible, the approach proposed by the social partners, which was that the Code should be short, its use voluntary and effective and that it should be capable of being used during different stages of collective bargaining.

Essentially, the Code proposes two things:

- that a *plan for follow-up* should be drawn up and out an *analysis of the remuneration system* and evaluate the data required to detect sexual discrimination in the pay structures so that remedies can be found,
- that negotiators at all levels, whether on the side of the employers or the unions, who are involved in the determination of pay systems, should carry
- implemented to eliminate any sexual discrimination evident in the pay structures.

[2]COM (94) 6 final

PART I
PARTIES CONCERNED

A. *Organisations*

The Code is principally aimed at employers regardless of whether they are from the public or private sector because the principle of equal pay for work of equal value must in the first instance be applied by employers, who are required to pay equal wages whenever work of equal value is being carried out by male and female workers and whenever a difference in pay cannot be explained or justified other than on the basis of the worker's sex.

It is worth noting the particularly important role played by the public authorities as employers. Indeed, the full application of the principle of equal pay in the public sector would have an added value by serving as a good example.

Businesses, are of course invited, in agreement with their staff and/or their representatives, to apply the measures proposed in the Code, in the manner most suited to their size and structure.

B. Partners in negotiation

The Code targets the social partners directly. Indeed, most pay scales are the result of collective bargaining at sectoral or intersectoral level. The Court of Justice of the European Communities has also stated on a number of occasions that collective agreements must respect the principle of equal pay for the same work or work of equal value.

The task is therefore one of helping the parties in wage negotiations to remove all direct or indirect discrimination from the collective agreements concerned, thereby obtaining equal recognition for the work of women and men when the job requirements to be met are equal.

Indeed it would be desirable if at this level and subject to any necessary adjustments, the type of approach proposed could also be applied in relation to analysis of pay structures and follow-up action.

C. Individuals

Finally, the Code also aims to assist women and men who believe their work is under-valued because of sexual discrimination to obtain the necessary information to resolve their problem through negotiation or, as a last resort, to bring the matter to the national courts.

It should be noted in this respect that the question of equal pay goes far beyond a mere study of pay structures within any one business, sector or group of sectors. It also requires action at national level not only on behalf of employers' and employees' associations but also by governments.

PART II

CONTENT OF PAY STRUCTURES

The study of the content of pay structures aims to reveal any possible under-valuation of work typically carried out by women in comparison with that typically carried out by men and vice-versa. To this end the employer must determine, preferably in agreement with the staff and/or their representatives, what useful pieces of information should be gathered and then evaluate this information to see if there are signs of any procedures and practices relating to pay which are at the root of instances of discrimination.

This study should comprise three phases. First the relevant information should be collected and then it should undergo a two-stage evaluation. The first stage would be to draw up a general table showing the sex and pay of workers, and then the second stage would consist in analysing those pay-related elements identified as potentially discriminatory.

A. The relevant information

Information relevant for the purposes of the analysis should be collected across the whole of the organisation's workforce. Pay analysis within one establishment or within an individual grading or bargaining structure is not adequate as problems of sex discrimination may well arise between employees who work at the same or separate establishments, across grading structures or in different bargaining units. The focus of the information collected will vary according to the structure of the company and its pay system. Some of the information set out below will not be relevant to some organisations. It is for the organisation to determine, in conjunction with its employees, what information is relevant and necessary for the analysis.

1. Pay arrangements and policies

Information about pay arrangements, policies and practices should be obtained from the organisation's rules, handbooks and collective agreements. This will vary from organisation to organisation but may include:
– job descriptions
– grading, classification and evaluation systems
– grading/classification criteria
– pay provisions of collective agreements
– rules governing entitlement to pay and other contractual benefits
– job evaluation system
– performance pay handbook (including competencies, skills-based systems)
– rules governing the operation of bonus and incentive schemes
– piece work or contract work pay arrangements

– information on the market situation of individual jobs where relevant.

It is important that information is also obtained on pay arrangements and pay practices which follow custom and practice as well as formal rules.

2. Employees

Information about employees should be obtained from personnel and payroll records to show:

– gender
– grade
– job title
– hours of work excluding breaks
– bargaining unit or collective agreement
– required entry qualification
– other relevant qualifications
– length of service with organisation
– length of service with other relevant organisations
– basic pay
– additional payments and contractual benefits

The information should include temporary staff as well as those who are on permanent contracts and any employees who work as home-workers/outworkers.

B. Assessing the general information

The first stage of the assessment of the information should be the establishment of a general picture on gender and pay. An analysis may reveal that the pay system rewards employees by reference to qualifications. It may be that the qualifications rewarded do not reflect the informal qualifications which women have acquired. For example, in some Member States sewing skills might not attract a certificate but sewing machinists could not undertake the work without such skills. The definition of qualifications may need to be reviewed and in some cases expanded. Are the qualifications necessary for the jobs performed?

Where a large organisation has a complex (different structures for different levels or job families) pay structure, a clear course of action to address discrimination identified may not emerge. Therefore the wage structure should be transparent.

The general picture will provide an overview of pay arrangements and will assist in the identification of areas for priority attention. Particular aspects of the pay system will require a greater depth of analysis.

Examples of key indicators of potential sex bias are given below:

- women have lower average earnings than men with the same job title.
- women have lower average earnings than men in the same grade.
- women in female dominated unskilled jobs are paid less than the lowest male dominated unskilled job.
- jobs predominantly occupied by women are graded or evaluated lower than jobs predominantly occupied by men at similar levels of effort, skill or responsibility.
- women are paid less than men with equivalent entry qualifications and length of service.
- where separate bargaining arrangements prevail within one organisation those dominated by men receive higher pay than other bargaining groups dominated by women.
- the majority of men and women are segregated by different grading, classification and evaluation systems.
- part-time or temporary workers, who are mainly women, have lower average hourly earnings than full-time or permanent employees in the same job or grade.
- part-time or temporary workers, who are mainly women, have access to fewer pay and other contractual benefits.
- different bonus arrangements, piece rate and other 'payments-by-result' systems, apply in different areas of production affecting disproportionately one gender.
- different bonus, piece rate and other 'payment by results' calculations apply to different jobs in the same department affecting disproportionately one gender.
- different overtime rates apply in different departments affecting disproportionately one gender.
- holiday entitlements vary between jobs in the same grade affecting disproportionately one gender.

Whilst the findings above do not in themselves mean that there is unlawful sex discrimination in the pay system, they all merit further investigation. Each element in the make-up of pay or in the entitlement to pay and other contractual benefits needs to be analysed to ensure that there is an objective justification which is not affected by the sex of the workers explaining the differences in pay.

C. *Particular aspects of the pay system*

Practices will vary from organisation to organisation and this will affect the outcome of the analysis. Set out below are examples of practices which might prove to be discriminatory together with guidance on how to address them. However, it should be stressed that these practices are only mentioned as examples and that it is in no case implied that they are to be found in all organisations.

1. Basic Pay

- Women are consistently appointed at lower points in a pay scale than men are.
- Women are paid less than male predecessors in the job.
- Women progress more slowly through incremental scales and/or seldom reach higher points.
- Men are paid more, by supplement or by a higher grading, because of 'recruitment and retention' problems.

2. Bonus/Performance Pay and Piece Rates

- Female and male manual workers receive the same basic pay but men have access to bonus earnings.
- Performance pay is only available to senior posts/full timers/employees covered by the appraisal system.
- Women consistently receive lower performance ratings than men.

3. Pay Benefits

A smaller percentage of women employees than men are covered by the organisation's pay benefits.

4. Part-time Workers

Part-time workers receive lower hourly pay rates or they are excluded from bonuses and benefits.

5. Job Classification, Grading, Evaluation and Skills/Competency-based System

Job evaluation, grading classification and skills/competency-based systems are mechanisms which are used in some Member States to determine the hierarchy or hierarchies of jobs in an organisation or group of undertakings as the basis for pay systems. The following comments are to assist those organisations which use such schemes to analyse them to check they do not inadvertently discriminate against typically female workers in particular. Pay systems based on such schemes may have been in place in organisations for many years, without any review and many incorporate features which contribute to the undervaluing of work undertaken by women.

a. Nature of the Organisation

What is the objective of the organisation? What is its nature? What services and/or products does it provide?

Asking these questions will contribute to a determination of whether the design of the scheme reflects the priorities of the organisation. It may transpire that by valuing certain elements in work the priority of the organisation is not reflected. For example, a scheme in a hospital which fails to value at all the care of patients but over-emphasises financial or engineering skills and responsibilities may require review.

b. Type of Scheme

Is the scheme capable of measuring the different elements in diverse work or does it rank jobs without such assessments?

Are different jobs covered by different schemes, for example one for manual and one for clerical workers, or are all jobs covered by the same scheme? In the latter case, is the system capable of evaluating evenly the work performed by different groups of employees?

Is it appropriate to the jobs covered?

Because of gender segregation in the labour market and the argument that traditional job evaluation and classification schemes are not capable of classifying inherently different work on a uniform scheme, often there has been no common yardstick for measuring typically male and female jobs. Schemes which do not cover certain types of predominantly female work obviously cannot determine whether such work may be equally demanding, albeit in different ways, as male work. The concept of equal pay for work of equal value requires the measurement of diverse work by reference to a common standard. Whilst this approach is not common, some organisations are attempting to integrate manual and clerical jobs into unified systems. If such a scheme is put in place it assists in the removal of sex bias normally associated with gender-segregated pay structures.

c. *Job Titles*

Are different job titles given where similar work is undertaken?

Different job titles may be given to the same or similar jobs distinguished only by the gender of the job holder eg: Storekeeper, Stores Assistant. This may have implications for status and pay levels.

d. *Job Content*

Do the job descriptions describe all the work of the jobs and of typically female jobs in particular?

Do the job descriptions accurately describe the content of the tasks performed? In particular, is traditionally female work adequately captured? Is attention drawn to aspects of women's work which have previously gone unrecognised?

Is the work content of jobs consistently described?

Job descriptions should be constant in format irrespective of the sex of the person carrying out the occupation. There are often inconsistencies in the way male and female work is described.

e. *Factors*

A factor in a formal job evaluation scheme is an element of a job which is defined and measured, such as skill or mental effort. A factor may in turn be divided into sub-factors which go into greater detail under a particular heading. Jobs to be evaluated are assessed against the factors and sub-factors chosen.

Have any significant job features been omitted?

Some factors may favour one sex only. It should be ensured that factors capture both male and female work.

Factors which are more likely to be present in female jobs may not be identified at all by a scheme and therefore not valued at all, for example caring skills and responsibilities, human relations skills, organisational skills/responsibilities, manual dexterity and/or co-ordination, etc. Categorising jobs by reference to light or heavy work or weighting different factors without taking account of other elements in female as opposed to male work impacts adversely on women.

Does the job classification based on factors, or the weighting of these factors, respond to objective criteria?

Classifying work by reference to formal qualifications alone can in some instances impact adversely on women. There are skills which cannot be learned by experience alone but which benefit from formal education and qualifications. However, the qualifications or skills which many women have gained are frequently not identified as qualities to be counted positively when classifying work in the labour market. For example, nurturing, cleaning and caring skills may be assumed in certain types of work and not rewarded in pay systems. A kindergarten nurse's training may be school-based and therefore less well rewarded than typically male jobs which may be apprenticeship based.

Formal qualifications are generally rewarded but those learnt through a different process are frequently ignored. For example, experience learned in the home or by example from another worker may not be credited in the payment system. Thus the basis on which training and qualifications are rewarded may need to be reviewed.

Further to this assessment, the determination of the pay rates to be attached to the final job evaluation should reflect the relativities of *actual* demands of the work not 'the rate for the job' which may be influenced by traditional sex-based assumptions of worth. Therefore women should attract the pay levels enjoyed by male occupations with which their work has been found to be equivalent.

CONCLUSION

The aim of the Code is to serve as a working tool for the greatest possible number of social actors who are likely to be in a position to further the principle of equal pay for women and men for work of equal value.

This initiative should therefore be seen as part of a dynamic follow-up exercise involving management and labour plus other parties concerned at all levels capable of ensuring both a wide dissemination and an effective use of the Code.

At European Union level and in the context of the Fourth Community Action Programme on equal opportunities for men and women (1996–2000), which was adopted by Council Decision 95/593/EEC[3], the will to mobilise all those who are concerned with the economic and social questions of everyday life as well as those who work in the legal sphere to focus on this problem has already been clearly expressed.

In the light of the recommendations by the European Parliament in its Report on the Memorandum on Equal Pay for Work of Equal Value (PE 213.161/final), adopted on 21 December 1995, the Commission in cooperation and/or jointly with the social partners and other appropriate authorities, will be able to develop further and/or support initiatives aimed at promoting such schemes as:

- campaigns to raise awareness and provide information on equal pay for work of equal value, targeting, in particular, employers, employees and/or their representatives, as well as the parties involved in collective bargaining;
- the training of experts who can study and propose practical solutions to resolve problems affecting equal pay;
- the greater involvement of women in the processes of collectively negotiated wage settlements;
- the identification, examination and exchange of best practice likely to enrich the Code by providing concrete examples of the type of measures that it proposes, as well as their practical implementation.

[3]OJ L 335, 30.12.1995 p.37

Bibliography

Allen, K.R. (1990) Compensation in context: adapting to the needs of the nineties, in *Benefits & Compensation International,* December.

Armstrong, M. (1995) *A handbook of personnel management practice*, Kogan Page, London.

Armstrong, M. and Brown, A. (1995) *The job evaluation handbook,* Institute of Personnel Development, London.

Armstrong, M. and Murlis, H. (1994) *Reward management: a handbook of remuneration strategy and practice,* Kogan Page, London.

Arvey, R.D. Sex bias in job evaluation procedures, *Personnel Psychology*, 39, pp. 35–335.

Bowey, A.M. and Lipton, T. Prof. (1982) *Managing salary and wage systems,* Gower Publishing Group, Aldershot.

CBI *Equal pay for work of equal value*, Report of the CBI Equal Value Group, London.

CBI (1985) *Job evaluation schemes free of sex bias,* Equal Opportunities Commission, London.

Commission of the European Communities (1996) A *code of practice on the implementation of equal pay for work of equal value for women and men*, COM(96) 336 final, Brussels.

Dessler, G. (1994) *Human resource management,* Prentice Hall, Englewood Cliffs, New Jersey.

EC 92 (1990*)* Are your compensation programs ready? in EC 92 *The impact on pay delivery* in B. Brooks, M.C. Haller and J.R. ViguiJ *Benefits & Compensation International,* January/February.

Flannery, T.P., Hofrichter, D.A. and Platten, P.R. (1996) *People, performance and pay,* The Hay Group, New York.

Foulkes, F.K. (1991) *Executive compensation,* Harvard Business School Press, Boston.

Gross, S.E. (1995) *Compensation for teams,* The Hay Group, New York.

Henderson, R.I. (1994) *Compensation Management,* Prentice Hall, Englewood, New Jersey.

Hewitt Associates (1990) *Total compensation management*, Blackwell Publishers, Oxford 1991.

Lawler, E. (1990) *Strategic pay,* Jossey-Bass Publishers, San Francisco.

Lawler, E. (1984) The strategic design of reward systems, in E.A. Fombrun *Strategic Human Resource Management,* Wiley & Sons, New York.

Pay and benefits sourcebook, Croner Publications Ltd, Kingston upon Thames.

Rock, M.L. and L.A . Berger (1991) *The compensation handbook,* McGraw-Hill, Inc., New York.

Spencer, L.M. and Spencer, S.M. (1993) *Competence at work,* John Wiley & Sons Inc., New York.

Index

References in *italic* indicate figures or tables